Media Track List

Audio and video can be found in the *Inside Listening and Speaking* Digital Download Center. Go to www.insidelisteningandspeaking.com. Click on the Video Center for streaming video. Click on the Audio Center and choose to stream or download ⬇ the audio file you select.

UNIT 1

Listening	Listen	ILS_L1_U1_Listen1
	Listen for Main Ideas	ILS_L1_U1_Listen1
	Apply A	ILS_L1_U1_Listen1
Speaking	Listen	ILS_L1_U1_Listen2
	Listen for Main Ideas	ILS_L1_U1_Listen2
	Apply A	ILS_L1_U1_Listen2
	Apply C	ILS_L1_U1_Listen2
Pronunciation	Learn A	ILS_L1_U1_Pron_LearnA
	Learn B	ILS_L1_U1_Pron_LearnB
	Apply A	ILS_L1_U1_Pron_ApplyA
End of Unit Task	B	ILS_L1_U1_End
	C	ILS_L1_U1_End

UNIT 2

Listening	Watch	ILS_L1_U2_Watch
	Listen for Main Ideas	ILS_L1_U2_Watch
	Apply A	ILS_L1_U2_Watch
Speaking	Listen	ILS_L1_U2_Listen
	Listen for Main Ideas	ILS_L1_U2_Listen
	Apply A	ILS_L1_U2_Listen
	Apply B	ILS_L1_U2_Listen
Pronunciation	Learn A	ILS_L1_U2_Pron_LearnA
	Learn B	ILS_L1_U2_Pron_LearnB
	Apply A	ILS_L1_U2_Pron_ApplyA
End of Unit Task	B	ILS_L1_U2_End

UNIT 3

Listening	Watch	ILS_L1_U3_Watch
	Listen for Main Ideas	ILS_L1_U3_Watch
	Apply A	ILS_L1_U3_Watch
Speaking	Listen	ILS_L1_U3_Listen
	Listen for Main Ideas	ILS_L1_U3_Listen
Pronunciation	Learn A	ILS_L1_U3_Pron_LearnA
	Learn B	ILS_L1_U3_Pron_LearnB
	Apply A	ILS_L1_U3_Pron_ApplyA
End of Unit Task	A	ILS_L1_U3_End

UNIT 4

Listening	Listen	ILS_L1_U4_Listen1
	Listen for Main Ideas	ILS_L1_U4_Listen1
	Apply B	ILS_L1_U4_Listen1
Speaking	Listen	ILS_L1_U4_Listen2
	Listen for Main Ideas	ILS_L1_U4_Listen2
	Apply A	ILS_L1_U4_Listen2
Pronunciation	Learn A	ILS_L1_U4_Pron_LearnA
	Learn B	ILS_L1_U4_Pron_LearnB
	Learn C	ILS_L1_U4_Pron_LearnC
	Apply A	ILS_L1_U4_Pron_ApplyA
	Apply B	ILS_L1_U4_Pron_ApplyB

UNIT 5

Listening	Watch	ILS_L1_U5_Watch
	Listen for Main Ideas	ILS_L1_U5_Watch
	Apply A	ILS_L1_U5_Watch
Speaking	Listen	ILS_L1_U5_Listen
	Listen for Main Ideas	ILS_L1_U5_Listen
	Apply A	ILS_L1_U5_Listen
	Apply B	ILS_L1_U5_Listen
Pronunciation	Learn A	ILS_L1_U5_Pron_LearnA
	Learn B	ILS_L1_U5_Pron_LearnB
	Apply A	ILS_L1_U5_Pron_ApplyA
End of Unit Task	B	ILS_L1_U5_End

UNIT 6

Listening	Listen	ILS_L1_U6_Listen1
	Listen for Main Ideas	ILS_L1_U6_Listen1
	Apply A	ILS_L1_U6_Listen1
Speaking	Listen	ILS_L1_U6_Listen2
	Listen for Main Ideas	ILS_L1_U6_Listen2
	Apply A	ILS_L1_U6_Listen2
Pronunciation	Learn A	ILS_L1_U6_Pron_LearnA
	Learn B	ILS_L1_U6_Pron_LearnB
	Learn C	ILS_L1_U6_Pron_LearnC
End of Unit Task	A	ILS_L1_U6_End

UNIT 7

Listening	Listen	ILS_L1_U7_Listen
	Listen for Main Ideas	ILS_L1_U7_Listen
	Apply A	ILS_L1_U7_Listen
	Apply B	ILS_L1_U7_Note_ApplyB
Speaking	Watch	ILS_L1_U7_Watch
	Listen for Main Ideas	ILS_L1_U7_Watch
	Apply A	ILS_L1_U7_Watch
Pronunciation	Learn A	ILS_L1_U7_Pron_LearnA
	Learn B	ILS_L1_U7_Pron_LearnB
	Learn C	ILS_L1_U7_Pron_LearnC
	Apply A	ILS_L1_U7_Pron_ApplyA
End of Unit Task	A	ILS_L1_U7_End

UNIT 8

Listening	Listen	ILS_L1_U8_Listen
	Listen for Main Ideas	ILS_L1_U8_Listen
	Apply A	ILS_L1_U8_LIsten
Speaking	Watch	ILS_L1_U8_Watch
	Listen for Main Ideas	ILS_L1_U8_Watch
	Apply A	ILS_L1_U8_Watch
Pronunciation	Learn A	ILS_L1_U8_Pron_LearnA
	Learn B	ILS_L1_U8_Pron_LearnB
	Apply A	ILS_L1_U8_Pron_ApplyA

UNIT 9

Listening	Watch	ILS_L1_U9_Watch
	Listen for Main Ideas	ILS_L1_U9_Watch
	Apply A	ILS_L1_U9_Watch
Speaking	Listen	ILS_L1_U9_Listen
	Listen for Main Ideas	ILS_L1_U9_Listen
	Apply A	ILS_L1_U9_Listen
	Apply B	ILS_L1_U9_Listen
Pronunciation	Learn A	ILS_L1_U9_Pron_LearnA
	Learn B	ILS_L1_U9_Pron_LearnB
	Apply A	ILS_L1_U9_Pron_ApplyA
End of Unit Task	B	ILS_L1_U9_End

UNIT 10

Listening	Watch	ILS_L1_U10_Watch
	Listen for Main Ideas	ILS_L1_U10_Watch
	Apply B	ILS_L1_U10_Watch
Speaking	Listen	ILS_L1_U10_Listen
	Listen for Main Ideas	ILS_L1_U10_Listen
	Apply B	ILS_L1_U10_Listen
Pronunciation	Learn A	ILS_L1_U10_Pron_LearnA
	Learn B	ILS_L1_U10_Pron_LearnB
	Learn C	ILS_L1_U10_Pron_LearnC

OXFORD
UNIVERSITY PRESS

198 Madison Avenue
New York, NY 10016 USA

Great Clarendon Street, Oxford, OX2 6DP, United Kingdom

Oxford University Press is a department of the University of Oxford.
It furthers the University's objective of excellence in research, scholarship,
and education by publishing worldwide. Oxford is a registered trade
mark of Oxford University Press in the UK and in certain other countries

Adult Content Director: Stephanie Karras
Publisher: Sharon Sargent
Managing Editor: Tracey Gibbins
Senior Development Editor: Anna Norris
Associate Editor: Rachael Xerri
Head of Digital, Design, and Production: Bridget O'Lavin
Executive Art and Design Manager: Maj-Britt Hagsted
Content Production Manager: Julie Armstrong
Design Project Manager: Mary Chandler
Image Manager: Trisha Masterson

ISBN: 978 0 19 471913 1

Printed in China

This book is printed on paper from certified and well-managed sources

ACKNOWLEDGEMENTS

*We would also like to thank the following for permission to reproduce the following
photographs:* **Cover**, Shooting Gallery Photography/Corbis; Peter Frank/
Corbis; Zocchi Roberto/Shutterstock; ValeStock/Shutterstock; Tischenko
Irina/Shutterstock; Louisanne/Shutterstock; Dobermaraner/Shutterstock;
Eliks/Shutterstock. **Interior,** Alamy pp. 16 (antique phrenology head/
VintageMedStock), 25 (running shoes/Sergio Azenha), 32 (Volkswagen
Beetle/Max Herman), 59 (playing video games/Blend Images), 61 (gray wolf/
Newman Mark), 68 (dandelion/Arterra Picture Library), 73 (Edison light bulb/
colin burt), 80 (Graphic designer/Wavebreak Media ltd), 88 (MRI imaging
scanner/Spaces Images), 100 (debris in reef/Michael Patrick O'Neill); Corbis
UK Ltd. pp. 47 (skateboarding/Mike McGill), 47 (girl/Rick Gomez), 97 (reef/
Jason Isley/Scubazoo/Science Faction); Getty Images pp. 4 (biking/Yellow Dog
Productions), 40 (men with laptop/Betsie Van der Meer), 44 (soccer player/
Tetra Images/Mike Kemp), 52 (children's camp/Hero Images), 64 (cane toad/
Julie Thurston), 92 (student/Jose Luis Pelaez Inc), 104 (hanging bridge/Kevin
Schafer), 107 (scuba diver with Palau Nautiluses/J.W.Alker), 109 (prosthetic/
John B. Carnett/Contributor); newscom.com pp. 56 (Google campus bike/
picture alliance/Ole Spata), 116 (artificial heart/CARMAT/MAXPPP/MAXPPP);
Oxford University Press p. 76 (variety of new technologies/Bacho); 112
(wheelchair/Ingram); Redux Pictures Archive p. 8 (Google self-driving car/
Jason Henry); Reuters Pictures p. 11 (foldable electric vehicle/Kim Hong-Ji);
Shutterstock pp. 1 (grass house/Dim Dimich), 13 (microscope/Africa Studio),
20 (mortar/Lukas Gojda), 28 (sale sign/Anton Havelaar), 37 (Facebook on tablet/
olegganko), 49 (foosball/Malyshev Oleg), 85 (MRI slide/Kondor83).

Acknowledgements

We would like to acknowledge the following individuals for their input during the development of the series:

Salam Affouneh
Higher Colleges of Technology
Abu Dhabi, U.A.E.

Kristin Bouton
Intensive English Institute
Illinois, U.S.A.

Nicole H. Carrasquel
Center for Multilingual Multicultural Studies
Florida, U.S.A.

Elaine Cockerham
Higher College of Technology
Muscat, Oman

Danielle Dilkes
CultureWorks English as a Second Language Inc.
Ontario, Canada

Susan Donaldson
Tacoma Community College
Washington, U.S.A

Penelope Doyle
Higher Colleges of Technology
Dubai, U.A.E.

Edward Roland Gray
Yonsei University
Seoul, South Korea

Melanie Golbert
Higher Colleges of Technology
Abu Dhabi, U.A.E.

Elise Harbin
Alabama Language Institute
Alabama, U.S.A.

Bill Hodges
University of Guelph
Ontario, Canada

David Daniel Howard
National Chiayi University
Chiayi

Leander Hughes
Saitama Daigaku
Saitama, Japan

James Ishler
Higher Colleges of Technology
Fujairah, U.A.E.

John Iveson
Sheridan College
Ontario, Canada

Alan Lanes
Higher Colleges of Technology
Dubai, U.A.E.

Corinne Marshall
Fanshawe College
Ontario, Canada

Christine Matta
College of DuPage
Illinois, U.S.A.

Beth Montag
University at Kearney
Nebraska, U.S.A.

Kevin Mueller
Tokyo International University
Saitama, Japan

Tracy Anne Munteanu
Higher Colleges of Technology
Fujairah, U.A.E.

Eileen O'Brien
Khalifa University of Science, Technology, and Research
Sharjah, U.A.E.

Jangyo Parsons
Kookmin University
Seoul, South Korea

John P. Racine
Dokkyo Daigaku
Soka City, Japan

Scott Rousseau
American University of Sharjah
Sharjah, U.A.E.

Jane Ryther
American River College
California, U.S.A

Kate Tindle
Zayed University
Dubai, U.A.E.

Melody Traylor
Higher Colleges of Technology
Fujairah, U.A.E.

John Vogels
Higher Colleges of Technology
Dubai, U.A.E.

Kelly Wharton
Fanshawe College
Ontario, Canada

Contents

The Inside Track to Academic Success

Student Books

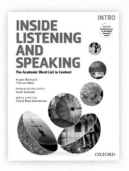   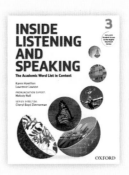 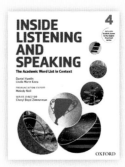

For additional student resources, visit: www.insidelisteningandspeaking.com.

iTools for all levels

The *Inside Listening and Speaking* iTools component is for use with a projector or interactive whiteboard.

Resources for whole-class presentation

> **Book-on-screen** focuses class on teaching points and facilitates classroom management.

> **Audio and video** at point of use facilitates engaging, dynamic lessons.

Resources for assessment and preparation

> Customizable Unit, Mid-term, and Final Tests evaluate student progress.

> Complete Answer Keys are provided.

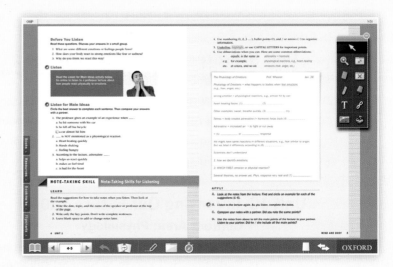

For additional instructor resources, visit:
www.oup.com/elt/teacher/insidelisteningandspeaking.

About *Inside Listening and Speaking*

Unit features

> **Explicit skills instruction** prepares students for academic listening

> **Authentic videos** from a variety of academic contexts engage and motivate students

> **Pronunciation instruction** ensures students are articulate, clear speakers

The Academic Word List and the Oxford 3000

Based on a corpus of 4.3 million words, the **Academic Word List (AWL)** is the most principled and widely accepted list of academic words. Compiled by Averil Coxhead in 2000, it was informed by academic materials across the academic disciplines.

The **Oxford 3000™** have been carefully selected by a group of language experts and experienced teachers as the most important and useful words to learn in English. The Oxford 3000 are based on the American English section of the Oxford English Corpus.

> **Oxford 3000 and Academic Word List vocabulary** is integrated throughout the unit and practiced in context through audio and video resources.

Explicit Skills Instruction

Before You Listen

Read these questions. Discuss your answers in a small group.

1. What are some environmental problems in your city or country?
2. What are some ways that cities can help the environment?
3. What does your city do to help or hurt the environment?

⊘ Listen

Read the Listen for Main Ideas activity below. Go online to listen to a lecture by Dr. Peter Jones about how eco-friendly cities are trying to help the environment.

⊘ Listen for Main Ideas

Mark each sentence as *T* (true) or *F* (false). Work with a partner. Restate false sentences to make them correct.

___T__ 1. Jones works with cities to help them become more eco-friendly.
_____ 2. He talks about five ways cities help the environment.
_____ 3. A building with a rooftop garden uses less electricity.
_____ 4. Wind can help cool a building.
_____ 5. In Copenhagen, Denmark, people get bus tickets when they recycle.
_____ 6. In Barcelona, Spain, they have one large bin for different kinds of trash.

NOTE-TAKING SKILL | Introduction to Note-Taking

LEARN

Taking notes is an important academic skill. Taking notes helps you to listen carefully and think about what you hear. Also, your notes can help you remember the lecture. When you take notes as you listen to lectures or presentations, follow these guidelines.

1. Take notes only on important points—not everything the speaker says. The speaker often shows important information by writing on the board and by repeating or emphasizing keywords. Sometimes the speaker will use numbers. For example, *There are two important reasons … . The third group is … .*
2. Don't write every word the speaker says. Use phrases or words instead of sentences.

3. Always use the same short forms and abbreviations. Here are some common abbreviations:

   + and; plus   e.g. for example
   = equals; is the same as   etc. et cetera; and so on
   > greater than; more important than → causes; leads to

4. Write the main idea or heading on the left. Indent examples, details, and explanations.
5. Leave space so you can add or correct notes later.
6. After listening, reread your notes. Add missing information. Underline or put a star next to the key points you want to remember.

Complete the three main topics or approaches the speaker talks about.

Eco-friendly cities — 3 approaches
1. Building _____
2. _____ less
3. _____

Discussion questions activate students' knowledge and prepare them to listen.

Comprehension activities help students understand the listening materials in preparation for academic skills instruction.

Listening and speaking skill instruction is linked to the academic content. **Apply** sections give students the opportunity to practice the skills in context.

High-Interest Media Content

About the Topic

Children play outside less now than they did 50 years ago. One reason is that schools often don't give children time to play. Another reason is that families are very busy. Parents often work and the children go to after-school activities.

Before You Watch

Read these questions. Discuss your answers in a small group.

1. How do most children spend their free time?
2. Do you think it is important for children to have a lot of time to play? Why or why not?
3. How has play changed in the last 30 years?

⬣ Watch

Read the Listen for Main Ideas activity below. Go online to watch the video about a children's camp with a nature theme.

⬣ Listen for Main Ideas

Check (✓) the ideas mentioned in the video.

____ 1. The children live in the city and need to see nature.

_✓_ 2. The children enjoy spending time outdoors.

____ 3. Parents think their children spend too much time on electronics.

____ 4. It's important for kids to meet other children from different places.

____ 5. Richard Louv thinks nature helps children to learn.

____ 6. Children can get better at art.

____ 7. The children can see animals.

NOTE-TAKING SKILL | Listening for Main Ideas

LEARN

When you are listening to a presentation or lecture, it is important to understand the main idea the speaker is trying to get across.

Speakers will often identify the main ideas of their speech by stating them at the beginning and end of their presentation.

Pronunciation Instruction

Pronunciation skill instruction is supported by audio resources to ensure students are articulate, clear speakers.

PRONUNCIATION SKILL   Intonation in Greetings

LEARN

Intonation is the rise and fall of your voice when you speak. Using direct address—that is, a person's name or title—in a conversation often requires rising intonation.

Direct address is used to greet someone or to get a person's attention. When it is used at the beginning of the sentence, there is a pause (|) following the person's name or title. When it is used at the end of the sentence, there is a pause (|) before the person's name or title.

A. Go online to listen to the sentences. Notice the pause and the rising intonation.

1. Ben, | what did you find out?
2. Hi, | Lidia.

B. Go online to listen to the sentences. When a speaker has a serious tone or message, the speaker may use falling intonation.

1. I don't think you should do that, | Ben.
2. Class, | take out your pencils for the test.

Students **learn and apply** pronunciation skills in the context of the academic topic.

APPLY

A. Go online to listen for the intonation. Draw an arrow showing the intonation. Then draw a line (|) to show a pause.

1. That's great, | Ben.

2. Charles, aren't you listening?

3. How about you, Charles?

4. Ben, please stop talking.

5. Grace, what do you think?

B. Greet your classmates. Use direct address when using the phrases in the box. Also use direct address to respond. Use appropriate rising intonation and pausing.

A: How's it going, Pam?
B: Great, | Tina. How are you?

Hey!	Good to see you.
How's everything?	Everything's great.
How are things with you?	Good, thanks for asking.
How's it going?	Very well, thank you.

Green Design

In this unit, you will

> learn about how cities can be eco-friendly.
> increase your understanding of the target academic words for this unit.

LISTENING AND SPEAKING SKILLS

> Introduction to Note-Taking
> Participating in a Group Discussion
> **PRONUNCIATION** Intonation in Greetings

Self-Assessment

Think about how well you know each target word, and check (✓) the appropriate column. I have…

TARGET WORDS	never seen this word before.	heard or seen the word but am not sure what it means.	heard or seen the word and understand what it means.	used the word confidently in *either* speaking or writing.
AWL				
🔑 affect				
🔑 alternative				
🔑 approach				
🔑 aware				
🔑 environment				
🔑 source				
🔑 transport				
🔑 vehicle				

🔑 Oxford 3000™ keywords

Vocabulary Activities

A. Complete the paragraph with the target words from the box. Be sure to use the correct form of the word.

approach	environment	awareness	source	transportation

Pollution, or dirty water and air, is a problem in many places. Cities around the world have different _approaches_ to dealing with pollution. Some cities
(1)

want people to recycle trash rather than throw it away. These cities try to

raise _____ by giving information or by calling attention to recycling
(2)

bins. Some cities try to lower air pollution by lowering the amount of gas

people use. These cities make sure they have good public _____,
(3)

such as buses and trains, so people don't have to drive. Sometimes the buses

and trains have a different design so they can use different _____ of
(4)

energy instead of gas. Lowering the amount of pollution is one way to help

the _____.
(5)

B. Write the examples from the box under each head in the chart. With a partner, add two more ideas to each column.

boats	electricity	oil	subways	trains	wind
buses	high temperatures	pollution	sun	trash	

Environmental problems	Sources of energy	Types of transportation
high temperatures		

C. Some of the target words have multiple meanings. Match the dictionary definitions on the left with the example sentences on the right.

approach (verb)

Definitions

_a_ 1. to come near or nearer to someone or something

___ 2. to speak to someone, usually in order to ask for something

___ 3. to begin to deal with a problem or a situation

___ 4. to come close to something in amount, level, or quality

Example Sentences

a. The man approached the animal very carefully.

b. He climbed a mountain that approached 20,000 feet.

c. They wanted to approach the problem together.

d. I approached the professor about changing classes.

approach (noun)

Definitions

___ 1. a way of dealing with someone or something

___ 2. the act of coming nearer to someone or something

___ 3. the road or path that leads to a place

Example Sentences

a. There are several approaches to the city.

b. Our city's approach to recycling is not working very well.

c. On its approach to the airport, the plane hit some birds.

D. With a partner, match each item with its source. Take turns making sentences with the information.

Source

_d_ 1. wind

Wind is a source of energy.

___ 2. the Internet

___ 3. cars

___ 4. fruits and vegetables

___ 5. jobs

Item

a. air pollution

b. vitamins

c. information

d. energy

e. income

About the Topic

The *environment* refers to the world around us—the air, the water, the plants, and the animals. As the world becomes more crowded with people, traffic, and buildings, it is harder to keep the environment clean and healthy. Engineers try to design things such as buildings and cars to be more eco-friendly.

Before You Listen

Read these questions. Discuss your answers in a small group.

1. What are some environmental problems in your city or country?
2. What are some ways that cities can help the environment?
3. What does your city do to help or hurt the environment?

Listen

Read the Listen for Main Ideas activity below.
Go online to listen to a lecture by Dr. Peter Jones
about how eco-friendly cities are trying to help
the environment.

Listen for Main Ideas

Mark each sentence as *T* (true) or *F* (false). Work with a partner. Restate false
sentences to make them correct.

_T_ 1. Jones works with cities to help them become more eco-friendly.

____ 2. He talks about five ways cities help the environment.

____ 3. A building with a rooftop garden uses less electricity.

____ 4. Wind can help cool a building.

____ 5. In Copenhagen, Denmark, people get bus tickets when they recycle.

____ 6. In Barcelona, Spain, they have one large bin for different kinds of trash.

NOTE-TAKING SKILL   Introduction to Note-Taking

LEARN

Taking notes is an important academic skill. Taking notes helps you to
listen carefully and think about what you hear. Also, your notes can help
you remember the lecture. When you take notes as you listen to lectures
or presentations, follow these guidelines.

1. Take notes only on important points—not everything the speaker says.
   The speaker often shows important information by writing on the board
   and by repeating or emphasizing keywords. Sometimes the speaker will
   use numbers. For example, *There are two important reasons ... . The third
   group is ... .*

2. Don't write every word the speaker says. Use phrases or words instead
   of sentences.

3. Always use the same short forms and abbreviations. Here are some common abbreviations:

+ and; plus   e.g. for example

= equals; is the same as   etc. et cetera; and so on

> greater than; more important than   → causes; leads to

4. Write the main idea or heading on the left. Indent examples, details, and explanations.

5. Leave space so you can add or correct notes later.

6. After listening, reread your notes. Add missing information. Underline or put a star next to the key points you want to remember.

Complete the three main topics or approaches the speaker talks about.

Eco-friendly cities — 3 approaches

1. Building _____
2. _____ less
3. _____

APPLY

A. Write down the three main topics from the notes above. Go online to listen to the lecture again. Write details and examples under each main topic. Use the following outline to help you organize your notes.

Eco-friendly cities — 3 approaches

1. Building _____
   - Rooftop gardens. Where: Malmo (Sweden), NY, Singapore
   - _____. Where: Singapore

2. _____ less
   - _____. Where: Copenhagen and _____.
   - _____. Where: Reykjavik
   - _____. Where: Curitiba, Brazil

3. _____
   - _____. Where: Curitiba
   - _____. Where: _____.
   - _____. Where: _____.

B. When you finish, use your notes to write 10 questions about the lecture.

What city uses wind to cool its buildings?

C. Work with a partner. Take turns asking and answering questions.

Vocabulary Activities

Word Form Chart			
Noun	**Verb**	**Adjective**	**Adverb**
alternative	_____	alternative	alternatively
approach	approach	approaching	_____
vehicle	_____	_____	_____

A. Work with a partner. Complete the paragraph using the correct form of the target words in the Word Form Chart. Use the words in parentheses to help you. Some words are used more than once.

The world may run out of oil one day. This __*approaching*__ oil shortage makes
   (1. coming)

many people worry. Most carmakers and car owners want to use less oil. So

companies are making cars that use _____ sources of fuel. Hybrid
                                       (2. different)

_____ use two forms of energy—gas and electricity. When on a
   (3. cars)

highway, the car uses gas. But in the city, it uses more electricity. Another

_____ for gas is cooking oil. This _____ to the fuel problem
   (4. possibility)   (5. way of dealing)

is eco-friendly. It uses old restaurant oil.

To *affect* something means to make a difference to something.

   The weather **affects** my moods. When it is raining, I am sad.

Affect is usually used as a verb. It sounds a lot like the noun *effect*. An *effect* is a result or something that happens because of something else.

   Rainy weather can have an **effect** on your feelings.

The two words are similar in meaning and sound, but different in word form.

to *affect* something = to have an *effect* on something

CORPUS

B. Match the word on the left with something it *affects* on the right. With a partner, take turns making sentences with the information.

_c_ 1. haircut

____ 2. smoking

____ 3. rooftop gardens

____ 4. recycling

____ 5. public transportation

a. the amount of trash

b. the temperature of the building

c. your appearance

d. your health

e. the number of cars on the road

The word *vehicle* usually refers to something that carries, or transports, people or things, such as a truck or a car.

> *The roads were crowded with too many* **vehicles.**

Sometimes *vehicle* refers to things that express ideas.

> *My writing is a* **vehicle** *for my feelings.*

A *vehicle* can also refer to songs, TV shows, etc. that show an actor or singer in a good way.

> *That song is a good* **vehicle** *for Shakira. It really shows how strong her voice is.*

CORPUS

C. With a partner, match each person to a good vehicle for his / her abilities.

_c_ 1. Adele

____ 2. President Obama

____ 3. Imran Kahn

____ 4. Mikhail Baryshnikov

____ 5. Isabel Allende

a. a ballet

b. a movie

c. a CD

d. a speech

e. a book

D. For each sentence, write N if the word *alternative* is a noun. Write Adj if *alternative* is an adjective.

_N_ 1. If we are going to reduce air pollution, we need alternatives to the use of fossil fuels such as gasoline.

____ 2. One alternative source of energy is hydrogen.

____ 3. Another alternative to fossil fuels is solar power.

____ 4. In addition, we can stop using personal vehicles. People can take alternative modes of transportation.

____ 5. Alternatives such as walking and bicycling not only reduce pollution, they help our health.

About the Topic

Car companies are always trying to make better cars. Sometimes better cars use less gas, sometimes they are more powerful, and sometimes they use new technology. The problem is that these cars are usually more expensive so many people don't buy them.

Before You Listen

Discuss these questions with a partner.

1. How are cars today different from cars 20 years ago?

2. What are some reasons for new car designs?

3. What is most important to you in a car?

Listen

Read the Listen for Main Ideas activity below. Go online to listen to four students talk about self-driving cars. They are going to present their ideas to the class later.

Listen for Main Ideas

Read the questions about driverless cars. Work with a partner to ask and answer the questions.

1. What are two types of self-driving or driverless cars?

2. Where are driverless cars used?

3. Are many people buying driverless cars?

4. What is the group's opinion of the cars at the end of the discussion?

SPEAKING SKILL   Participating in a Group Discussion

LEARN

Group discussions are often part of class or homework assignments. They are a good way to talk about your ideas and practice what you learn. For successful group discussions, follow these guidelines:

1. Prepare. If you know what the discussion will be about, find some information first. Read about the topic or review class notes.

2. Take notes before and during the discussion.

3. Listen. When other people speak, pay attention to what they say.

4. Ask questions to get more information.

5. Participate. Don't just sit there quietly. Share your ideas. Everyone can learn from others in the group.

6. Be polite. Use polite language (for example, *thanks, excuse me, I'm sorry, please*).

7. Don't talk too much.

A. Go online to listen to the audio again. Check (✓) the person who does each thing.

	Ben	Lidia	Charles	Grace
Doesn't prepare				
Doesn't listen well				
Doesn't participate				
Isn't polite				
Talks too much				

B. One way to have a good group discussion is to assign roles. Read about each role below. Write the name of the person in each role in the listening.

1. Leader: This person often starts the discussion. He / She asks other members for their ideas. _____

2. Recorder: This person takes notes. He / She writes down the important things people say. _____

3. Reporter: This person tells the class about the group's discussion. _____

C. Go online to listen to the audio again. Take notes about the good and bad points of driverless cars. Add your own ideas to the chart.

Good points	Bad points

D. Follow the guidelines for participating in a group discussion. Work in a group of three and assign roles. Answer the questions below. Share your ideas with the class.

1. What are some good points about self-driving cars?
2. What are some possible problems with such cars?
3. Do you think that these cars will help the environment? Why or why not?
4. Do you think these cars will be popular in the next five years? Why or why not?

LEARN

Intonation is the rise and fall of your voice when you speak. Using direct address—that is, a person's name or title—in a conversation often requires rising intonation.

Direct address is used to greet someone or to get a person's attention. When it is used at the beginning of the sentence, there is a pause (|) following the person's name or title. When it is used at the end of the sentence, there is a pause (|) before the person's name or title.

A. Go online to listen to the sentences. Notice the pause and the rising intonation.

1. Ben, | what did you find out?
2. Hi, | Lidia.

B. Go online to listen to the sentences. When a speaker has a serious tone or message, the speaker may use falling intonation.

1. I don't think you should do that, | Ben.
2. Class, | take out your pencils for the test.

APPLY

A. Go online to listen for the intonation. Draw an arrow showing the intonation. Then draw a line (|) to show a pause.

1. That's great, | Ben.

2. Charles, aren't you listening?

3. How about you, Charles?

4. Ben, please stop talking.

5. Grace, what do you think?

B. Greet your classmates. Use direct address when using the phrases in the box. Also use direct address to respond. Use appropriate rising intonation and pausing.

A: How's it going, Pam?
B: Great, | Tina. How are you?

Hey!	Good to see you.
How's everything?	Everything's great.
How are things with you?	Good, thanks for asking.
How's it going?	Very well, thank you.

C. Invite a partner to join you in an activity. Practice direct address with rising intonation by politely saying you can't make it, using the phrases in the box. Use appropriate falling intonation and pausing.

I have to …

I already made plans …

I'm busy …

I'm sorry, …

> A: *Do you want to come to the movies with me?*
>
> B: *I can't, | Jean. I have to write a paper.*

End of Unit Task

In this unit, you learned how to take notes and to participate in group discussions. Review these skills by taking notes in a new group discussion and share your ideas. As you review, make sure you correctly identify the topic discussed.

A. Look at the Japanese folding car below. With a partner, discuss some good things about this design. Then discuss some possible problems.

B. Listen to the podcast about eco-friendly cars. Check (✓) the things the speaker talks about.

- ☐ hybrid cars
- ☐ electric cars
- ☐ driverless cars
- ☐ cars with sails
- ☐ cars that use oil

- ☐ cars that use coffee
- ☐ cars that burn wood
- ☐ cars that use the sun
- ☐ very small cars
- ☐ folding cars

C. Go online to listen again and take notes.

- Compare notes with two other students. What headings did you use? What details did you add?

D. Work in groups of three. Assign the following roles:

- Group leader
- Recorder
- Reporter

List the types of cars the speaker discusses in the podcast. For each one, list good and bad points about it. The group leader makes sure everyone participates.

Type of car	Good points (+)	Bad points (−)

E. As a group, choose the best car design. The recorder will make sure that he / she has all the notes from the discussion. The reporter presents the group's idea to the class.

F. As you listen to the ideas from the other groups, take notes.

Self-Assessment		
Yes	**No**	
☐	☐	I successfully identified what the speaker talked about.
☐	☐	I successfully took notes, adding headings and details.
☐	☐	I participated in a group discussion and shared ideas with the class.
☐	☐	I can use correct intonation for direct address.
☐	☐	I can correctly use the target vocabulary words from the unit.

Discussion Questions

With a partner or in a small group, discuss the following questions.

1. What are some ways you could make your city more eco-friendly?
2. Is it the government's or private citizens' job to make a city eco-friendly?
3. Do you think self-driving cars are safe?

Making Medicines

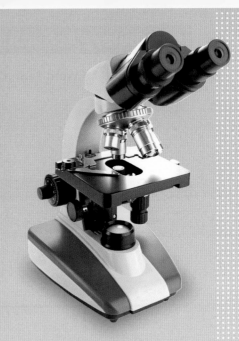

In this unit, you will

> learn about the history of different types of medicine.

> increase your understanding of the target academic words for this unit.

LISTENING AND SPEAKING SKILLS

> Categorizing Names and Dates

> Asking For and Giving Examples

> **PRONUNCIATION** Intonation in Statements and Questions

Self-Assessment

Think about how well you know each target word, and check (✓) the appropriate column. I have…

TARGET WORDS	never seen this word before.	heard or seen this word but am not sure what it means.	heard or seen the word and understand what it means.	used the word confidently in *either* speaking or writing.
AWL				
🔑 benefit				
🔑 demonstrate				
🔑 legal				
🔑 medical				
🔑 method				
🔑 participate				
🔑 process				
🔑 professional				

🔑 Oxford 3000™ keywords

Vocabulary Activities

A. Complete the Word Form Chart below with the correct form of the target words.

legal	legality	medically	method	process
legally	medical	medicine	methodical	processed

Word Form Chart			
Noun	**Verb**	**Adjective**	**Adverb**
legality			

B. Complete the sentences with the target words from the Word Form Chart in activity A. Be sure to use the correct form and tense of each word.

1. It is not ___*legal*___ to sell new drugs without testing them.
   (1)

2. The series of steps that must be followed to test new drugs is a lengthy

   _____ .
   (2)

3. People trust the _____ community to suggest medicine that is safe.
   (3)

4. Another _____ , or way that people stay healthy, is through vaccines.
   (4)

5. Vaccines are drugs that stop people from getting a sickness. Vaccines are

   _____ in special places.
   (5)

6. The new _____ of testing drugs is _____ very safe.
   (6)   (7)

7. She was very _____ in her scientific research. She followed each step
   (8)

   slowly and carefully.

The noun *process* means a series of steps or actions to reach a particular end.

*The college application **process** can take up to two years.*

It can also refer to a natural series of changes.

*Slowing down is a part of the aging **process**.*

The verb *process* means to follow a series of steps to change or save something. It often takes place in a factory or lab.

*Colleges **process** a lot of applications during the fall.*

*We **process** milk to make it safer to drink.*

The verb *process* can also mean to walk, march, or move in a line of people or cars.

*The students **processed** into the auditorium for graduation.*

When we use *process* as a noun, the stress is on the first syllable (**pro** cess). When used as a verb, the stress is on the second syllable (pro **cess**).

CORPUS

C. With a partner, decide which of these sentences make sense. Write *Y* (yes) or *N* (no). Explain your reasons.

___N___ 1. The boy processed into his bedroom. *(One person can't process.)*

_____ 2. I always follow the same process to make my morning coffee.

_____ 3. Drug companies process drugs in labs.

_____ 4. Mary used processed cheese for her sandwich.

_____ 5. The store processed my credit card payment.

_____ 6. You can get a car to process.

D. With a partner, discuss which things are legal in your country.

- driving a car at age 16
- getting married at age 15
- spitting in public
- owning a gun
- giving unusual names to your children

About the Topic

People have been searching for medicine to treat pain and sickness for hundreds of years. Today, drug companies do a lot of research to be sure that new drugs are a safe and effective way to fight diseases. It often takes many years for a drug to become available for people to buy. This was not always true.

Before You Watch

Read these questions. Discuss your answers in a small group.

1. What do you do to feel better when you are sick?
2. Do you take any medicines regularly?
3. Do you think most medicines are safe?

◑ Watch

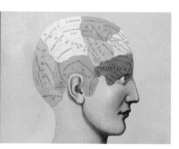

Read the Listen for Main Ideas activity below. Go online to watch the presentation on the history of medicine.

◑ Listen for Main Ideas

Mark each sentence as *T* (true) or *F* (false). Work with a partner. Restate false sentences to make them correct.

_T_ 1. Plant leaves were one of the earliest types of medicine.

___ 2. Explorers brought quinine from Asia to other parts of the world.

___ 3. The first modern pills were developed by William Upjohn.

___ 4. Most governments require that medicines come with written instructions.

___ 5. A vaccine works by killing the bacteria that causes disease.

LEARN

When the topic of a lecture is about the history of something, you will probably hear a lot of names and dates. One way to take notes is to make a chart or table with headings like this:

When? (dates)	Who? (names)	What? (event)
	Barnabé de Cobo	
1800s		put medicine in pills
	Edward Jenner	
		Rabies vaccine
		Polio vaccine
1906		

Listen for numbers and names to complete the first two columns. If you miss the detail, you can ask the instructor or classmates for the information, using questions like the ones below.

"When did … ?"

"In what year did … ?"

"What drug did they develop in _____?"

"Who invented _____?"

"Who first used a vaccine?"

APPLY

A. Watch the video again. Write the following events in the correct places in the chart. Add names and dates if appropriate and cross out events as you use them.

Events:
vaccine for smallpox
drug for malaria
government control of drugs in the USA
~~vaccine for rabies~~

B. Write questions about dates, events, and people mentioned in the video. Use *what*, *who*, and *when*.

C. Work with a partner. Take turns asking and answering the questions about the video. Then retell key ideas from the clip.

Vocabulary Activities

Word Form Chart			
Noun	**Verb**	**Adjective**	**Adverb**
benefit	benefit	beneficial	_____
demonstration demonstrator	demonstrate	demonstrable demonstrative	demonstratively
participant (person) participation (action)	participate	_____	_____
professional (person)	_____	professional	professionally

A. Complete the paragraph with target words from the Word Form Chart. Make sure to use the correct form of each word.

My mother had cancer 15 years ago. Because cancer is such a difficult

disease, she decided to take part, or ___participate___ in, a study. She had
                                        (1)

different kinds of treatment, including surgery, and then some powerful

medicine. As a _____ in the study, she worked with a number of
                   (2)

medical _____, not just one doctor. The medicine caused nausea,
              (3)

or a sick feeling in her stomach. A nurse told her that herbal tea made from

different plants might help because one _____ of certain herbs is to
                                            (4)

help with nausea. My mother worked with a nutritionist who taught her about

healthy foods. Certain fruits and vegetables are _____ in fighting
                                                       (5)

cancer. My mother was glad she was in the study because it _____
                                                                (6)

that a particular medicine could really help people with cancer.

B. Write the words from the box below under the correct heading in the chart on page 19. Add two more ideas.

architects	chess club members	engineers	lower weight	soccer players
Boy Scouts	doctors	good health	lower stress	teachers

Benefits of exercise	Participants in after-school activities	Professionals
good health		

There are two noun forms of the verb *participate*. The noun *participant* refers to the people who take part in an activity.

*The first clinical trial of the new drug included 300 **participants**.*

The noun *participation* refers to the act of taking part in something.

*Many teachers welcome student **participation** in classroom discussions.*

CORPUS

C. Choose an antonym and synonym for each target word from the list of words below.

	synonym	**antonym**	
1. benefit	_help_	_harm_	(help / win / lose / harm)
2. demonstrate	_____	_____	(answer / hide / find / show)
3. participate	_____	_____	(finish / lead / take part / watch)
4. professional	_____	_____	(boring / skilled / strong / untrained)

There are two adjective forms of the verb *demonstrate*. The adjective *demonstrable* means something "can be shown or proved."

*The drug had no **demonstrable** effect on the cancer.*

The adjective *demonstrative* means the quality of "showing feelings openly, especially feelings of affection."

*Some people are more **demonstrative** than others.*

CORPUS

D. Circle the correct form of the target words in each sentence.

Dr. Hanna does research for a drug company. He is working on a drug to

treat high blood pressure. He's tried it on mice and the drug had a

1. **demonstrable** / **demonstrative** effect. However, now he is testing the

medicine on people. He got two thousand 2. **participation** / **participants** to agree to take part. They signed releases that said they understood the dangers of the study. This is an important step because he has to show that their 3. **participation / participant** is informed and that they are aware of the risks. Although the 4. **participants / participations** have only been on the medicine for six months, they are already showing 5. **demonstrative / demonstrable** improvement. He is not usually 6. **demonstrative / demonstrable**, but he cried in happiness at the news conference.

About the Topic

Some people go to see a doctor when they get sick. But other people try to treat the problem in other ways. They might do the same thing their grandmother or mother used to do. Different cultures have different kinds of remedies, or solutions, for medical problems.

Before You Listen

Discuss these questions with a partner.

1. People don't always go to the doctor when they are sick. What are some other ways they deal with sickness?
2. How do people in your country deal with medical problems?
3. How do you decide what to do when you or a family member is sick?

Listen

Read the Listen for Main Ideas activity below. Go online to listen to three students discuss alternative medicine.

Listen for Main Ideas

Read the questions about the different methods of getting healthy. Work with a partner to ask and answer these questions.

1. What is one way alternative medicine is different from regular medicine?
2. What are three examples of alternative medicine?
3. What can lower stress?
4. What treatments help pain?
5. How can scientists demonstrate that alternative medicine works?

LEARN

With a study group, you can discuss what you learned in class, review your notes, and confirm that you understood what the professor said. To do this, you will need to ask for and give your classmates examples. Read the phrases for *asking for* and *giving examples*.

Asking for examples	Giving examples
☐ Can / Could you give me an example?	☐ For example, ...
☐ For example?	☐ For instance, ...
☐ For instance?	☐ ... like ...
☐ Like what?	☐ ... such as ...
☐ Such as?	

APPLY

A. Go online to listen to the audio again. In the chart above, check (✓) the phrases you hear that ask for or give examples. Compare your phrases with a partner and add any phrases you missed.

B. Listen to the audio again. List examples of the treatments for illness that you hear mentioned. Then add two or three of your own ideas.

C. Work with a partner. Take turns asking for and giving examples. Use the ideas in the chart.

A: What's an example of a new way to treat illness?

B: Eating some foods, such as garlic, will help illness.

LEARN

Statements and *wh-* questions require falling intonation. *Yes / No* questions require rising intonation.

A. Go online to listen to the statements and *wh-* questions. Notice the falling intonation.

1. Thanks for meeting today.
2. I thought it was pretty interesting.
3. How can they do that?
4. What is it used for?

B. Go online to listen to the *yes / no* questions. Notice the rising intonation.

1. Did I miss a lot?
2. Can you give me an example?

APPLY

A. Go online to listen to six sentences. Circle *rising* if the end of the sentence has rising intonation or *falling* if the end of the sentence has falling intonation.

1. (rising)	falling		4. rising	falling
2. rising	falling		5. rising	falling
3. rising	falling		6. rising	falling

B. With a partner, say the sentences in Learn, activities A and B with the appropriate rising or falling intonation. Check that your partner is using the right intonation.

C. With a partner, ask three questions about what you can do to relieve stress. Include both *yes / no* and *wh-* questions. Respond to your partner's questions with a statement. Use appropriate rising or falling intonation.

A: Do you like to do yoga to relieve stress?

B: I prefer to play basketball.

End of Unit Task

In this unit, you learned how to categorize information. You also learned how to ask for and give examples in a group discussion. Review these skills by taking notes on a new listening and by discussing topics in medicine.

A. Read about antibiotics below. Look up the words you don't know in a dictionary.

Most diseases or illnesses are caused by an unwanted virus or bacteria entering and attacking our bodies. We can treat bacterial illnesses with antibiotics. Penicillin is one of the first and most used antibiotic medicines.

B. Listen to the presentation on the history of penicillin. Take notes.

When?	Who?	What?
	Dr. Fleming	
		published studies of mold

C. Think of four examples of a time when you discovered something by accident or not on purpose. This could be a place, a food, a person you met, or a discovery you made.

D. Prepare a two-minute presentation. Discuss all of the following aspects of your topic. Categorize the information.

My accidental experience		
When?	Who?	What?

E. Work with a small group. Take turns presenting your topics. Ask for and give examples.

Self-Assessment		
Yes	**No**	
☐	☐	I successfully categorized information in my notes.
☐	☐	I successfully used a graphic organizer to prepare for a presentation.
☐	☐	I asked for examples in a group discussion.
☐	☐	I gave examples about my topic.
☐	☐	I can use appropriate intonation in *wh-* and *yes / no* questions.
☐	☐	I can correctly use the target vocabulary words from the unit.

Discussion Questions

With a partner or in a small group, discuss the following questions.

1. What is the most important drug or vaccine ever made?

2. What medicine do you think the world needs most?

3. What tests do you think need to be done to consider a medicine safe and effective?

Subliminal Messaging

In this unit, you will

> learn about marketing and how colors affect sales.

> understand how ads work.

> increase your understanding of the target academic words for this unit.

LISTENING AND SPEAKING SKILLS

> Understanding Ordinal Numbers and Percentages

> Using Statistics in a Short Speech

> **PRONUNCIATION** Listing Items in a Series

Self-Assessment

Think about how well you know each target word, and check (✓) the appropriate column. I have…

TARGET WORDS	never seen this word before.	heard or seen the word but am not sure what it means.	seen or heard the word and understand what it means.	used the word confidently in *either* speaking or writing.
AWL				
🔑 analyze				
🔑 communicate				
🔑 identify				
🔑 image				
🔑 percent				
🔑 primary				
🔑 react				
🔑 summary				

🔑 Oxford 3000™ keywords

Vocabulary Activities

A. Complete the paragraph with the target words from the box.

image	primary	percent	reaction

Think about a product you bought recently. Was it a pair of running shoes,

or a cell phone, or a car? Why did you buy it? Maybe because you like the

brand (e.g., Nike). Maybe because you liked the price. The most important,

or ___*primary*___ reason why I buy something is the way it looks, or its
        (1)

_____. I like beautiful things, so that's what I pay attention to. When
        (2)

I look at something, I have an immediate _____. I know right away if
                                                    (3)

I like it or not. This feeling is very strong, or powerful. If the product doesn't

look good, I really don't like it. I don't think I'm alone. I bet most people,

maybe 80 _____ feel the same way.
                (4)

B. Some target words have multiple meanings. For the target words below, match
the dictionary definitions on the left with the example sentences on the right.

primary (adjective)

Definitions

_a_ 1. the most important

___ 2. the early grades in school

___ 3. a color that is not mixed with
        another color.

Example Sentences

a. The primary purpose of recycling
    is to reduce trash.

b. Blue is a primary color, but green
    is a mixture of blue and yellow.

c. In the United States, elementary
    school students are usually 10
    years old or younger.

image (noun)	

Definitions

Example Sentences

____ 1. A picture on paper, in a mirror, or made by a camera and seen on a computer.

a. He is the image of his father.

____ 2. a picture in people's minds of someone or something

b. Do you have any images of tigers? I want to add one to my presentation.

____ 3. a person or thing that looks like another person or thing

c. The car is an image of wealth and luxury.

____ 4. the general impression people have of a product, person, or organization

d. I have an image of me driving a Jaguar.

C. One meaning of *react* is to do or say something because something has happened. With a partner, answer this question: Do you react positively (+) or negatively (–) to the following?

__+__ 1. getting a good grade on a test

____ 2. finishing second in a race

____ 3. a product that is eco-friendly

____ 4. rain

____ 5. a high price on something I like

The noun *percent* (%) means one part of 100. It is used with a specific number.

> Twenty **percent** of the student population is sick.

The noun *percentage* is used without a number. Percentage takes the singular noun form [*is, was*].

> What **percentage** of sales is due to the brand's color?

CORPUS

D. Write *percent* or *percentage* on the lines below to accurately complete each sentence.

1. Of all the top companies, a large ___percentage___ uses the colors blue, red, or black.

2. Can you tell me the _____ of brands that uses black?

3. The number of people in China is just under 20 _____ of the world's population.

4. I can't give an exact _____, but our sales are up.

5. Only 35 _____ of hybrid owners plan to buy another hybrid.

About the Topic

Companies want to sell as many products as they can. They spend a lot of money on marketing research to find out what makes a customer want to buy something. Surprisingly, their results show that many people choose to buy something based on the same reasons.

Before You Watch

Read these questions. Discuss your answers in a small group.

1. What colors do you like? Why?

2. How do different colors make you feel?

3. Think of a few brand names. What colors are used in the advertising of these brands?

Watch

Read the Listen for Main Ideas activity below. Go online to watch a presentation about how the color of a product affects what we think and how we feel about the product, and of course, its sales.

Listen for Main Ideas

Read the statements about the video. Circle the best answer to complete the statements. Then work with a partner and compare your answers.

1. Colors affect how people (feel) / talk about a product.

2. Red means **friendliness / energy**.

3. If you want to show happiness, you should choose **blue / yellow**.

4. Many **drink / car** companies use black or silver.

5. Most of the top brands use blue, red, black, or **yellow / orange**.

6. A customer who **doesn't plan to buy anything / wants to save money** likes the color green.

7. People in different countries often react to colors **in different ways / in the same way**.

LISTENING SKILL   Understanding Ordinal Numbers and Percentages

LEARN

It's important to understand numbers that are said as words. We use *ordinal numbers* such as *first, second, third,* and *tenth* to give examples and reasons. We also use them to give the order of events, or the order in a list.

First, companies can use color to tell something about their product.

We use *ordinal numbers* even when we don't list the items in the correct order.

The second most popular color is red. What do you think the first is?

Speakers often use *percentages* to talk about research, particularly in science and business. *Percentages* are always part of 100. We use *percent* after the number.

Ten percent preferred the yellow car.
Thirty-five percent of the people chose the green one.

APPLY

A. Go online to watch the video and listen again. Complete the outline with information from the lecture. Compare your outline with a partner.

How Colors Affect Sales

What colors mean
  Blue:
  Red: _____
  Yellow: _____
  Orange: _____
  Green: _____

The importance of looks
  Image: _____ % think it's important
  Color: _____ % say it's the primary reason they buy a product
  Examples:
  _____
  _____

Top brands
  Use 1 or 2 colors: _____ %
  Most popular:
  1. _____ , _____ %
  2. _____ , _____ %
  3. _____ , _____ %
  4. _____ , _____ %

Vocabulary Activities

A. Complete the paragraph with the target words from the box below. Be sure to use the correct form of the words.

analyze	communicate	identify	summary

Some colleges have courses on the media—television, newspapers, advertisements—in order to help students think more carefully about what they see and hear. In these courses, students learn to ___analyze___, or

(1)

take apart, look at, and think about, the messages they see in the media.

Students _____, or find and name, the different parts of the message.

(2)

For example, an ad _____ many things to readers. It tells about the

(3)

product, the company, and even the customer. Most media only give us a

_____ of what is important. They don't tell us everything, only what

(4)

they think we need to know. That is why these courses are so important.

The verb *communicate* means "to exchange information, news, ideas, etc. with somebody."

> We **communicate** mostly by text messages.

It can also mean "to make your ideas, feelings, etc. known to other people so that they understand them" or "to have a good relationship because you are able to understand and talk about people's thoughts and feelings."

> She is good at **communicating** her ideas to a group.

Communicate can also mean to pass a disease from one person to another.

> Some diseases are **communicated** through dirty water.

CORPUS

B. Match each of the following with the way they communicate.

_d_ 1. A company and customer   a. a song

___ 2. Two teenagers   b. a speech

___ 3. Two birds   c. text messages

___ 4. A musician and an audience   d. ads

___ 5. The president and people   e. music

The verb *identify* means "to recognize something or someone and be able to say who or what it is."

*I bought a pink suitcase so I can **identify** it easily at the airport.*

It can also mean "to find or discover somebody or something."

*The scientist **identified** a new disease.*

CORPUS

C. What do you think the people below identify? Complete the sentences using the phrases in the box.

the driver responsible	if an image is pleasing to look at	causes of pollution
	the number of products sold last year	works of art

1. Environmental scientists identify _____ *causes of pollution* _____.

2. Witnesses to an accident identify _____.

3. Advertising surveys identify _____.

4. The sales report identifies _____.

5. Museum experts identify _____.

The noun *summary* means a short statement that gives only the main idea—not details.

*You can find a **summary** of the report on the website.*

The verb *summarize* means to give a summary, or a short statement of the main points.

*At the end of the presentation, he **summarized** the important parts of an ad.*

CORPUS

D. Complete the sentences below with the correct form of *summary*.

1. At the end of your presentation, you should __*summarize*__ your main points.

2. In most movie reviews, the writer gives a _____ of the story.

3. The report _____ our sales for last year.

4. If you look at the information, you can find a _____ of the research, but it doesn't give any details.

About the Topic

One way that companies market their products is through advertising, such as commercials on television or ads in newspapers and online. Advertising often costs a lot of money. Companies usually pay a professional to design and create the ad. Then the company has to pay to put it on TV, in print, or online.

Before You Listen

Read these questions. Discuss your answers in a small group.

1. What kind of ads do you see every day?
2. What are some ads you think are good?
3. What makes an ad good?

Listen

Read the Listen for Main Ideas activity below. Go online to listen to a presentation about the different parts of ads and why they make us want to buy.

Listen for Main Ideas

Work with a partner and answer the questions.

1. How many ads do we see in a day?
2. Where do we see ads?
3. Which kind of ad is growing the fastest?
4. In addition to color, what is another part of the ad that is important?
5. Ads focus on needs people have. What is one of these needs?

PRESENTATION SKILL | Statistics in a Short Speech

LEARN

Using statistics and other numbers is an effective way to support ideas in speeches or presentations. Here are some ways to express statistics.

Numbers	Percentages	Fractions	Other expressions of quantity
Two hundred and fifty (250)	Ninety percent (90%)	Nine tenths (9/10)	Nearly all
Five thousand (5,000)	Seventy-five percent (75%)	Three quarters (3/4)	Most
Three and a half billion (3,500,000,000)	Fifty percent (50%)	Half (1/2)	More than half Less than half
Six point five million (6,500,000)	Thirty-three percent (33%)	One-third (1/3)	About a quarter

APPLY

A. Read the sentences from the presentations on marketing. For each, make a new sentence using a different way to express numbers.

1. About 20 years ago, people saw around 2,000 ads in a day. Now, if you read newspapers, watch TV, and go online, you will see more than 5,000 ads a day.

   About 20 years ago, people saw less than half the number of ads in a day as they do now.

2. Out of all the money put towards online advertising, the most was spent in North America, at more than 40% of the worldwide spending, followed by Western Europe at 28%, and then Asia at 25%.

3. In 2012, about $145 billion was spent on ads: $80 billion on TV ads, $40 billion on print, and $40 billion on online ads.

B. Work with a partner. Each choose one graph or chart below. Prepare a short presentation about the information in one of the charts. Use numbers and statistics in your presentation to your partner.

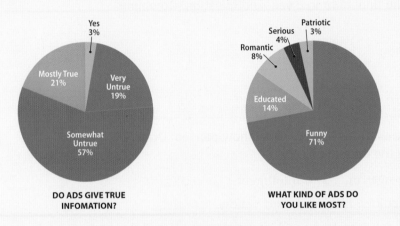

DO ADS GIVE TRUE INFOMATION?

Yes 3%
Mostly True 21%
Very Untrue 19%
Somewhat Untrue 57%

WHAT KIND OF ADS DO YOU LIKE MOST?

Patriotic 3%
Serious 4%
Romantic 8%
Educated 14%
Funny 71%

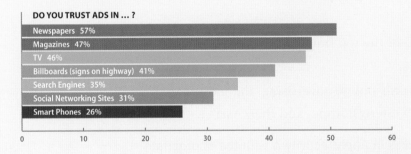

DO YOU TRUST ADS IN ... ?

Newspapers 57%
Magazines 47%
TV 46%
Billboards (signs on highway) 41%
Search Engines 35%
Social Networking Sites 31%
Smart Phones 26%

0   10   20   30   40   50   60

C. As you listen to your partner present the information, check that the statistics are correct by comparing your notes to the charts.

LEARN

When a you talk about a list of items, use rising intonation to let the listener know more items will be listed. Use rising intonation for each item until the final item. For the final item, use falling intonation. After each item, insert a pause (|).

A. Go online to listen to the sentences. Notice the intonation and the pauses between the items.

1. There are many parts to an ad including color, | mood, | shapes, | and story.

2. If you read newspapers, | watch TV, | and go online, | you will see more than 5,000 ads a day.

3. We trust blue, | yellow makes us happy, | and red makes us feel energy and danger.

B. Notice the rising intonation on the final item in a *yes / no* question. Go online to listen.

Is it | sad?

APPLY

A. Go online to listen to the sentences. Draw lines (|) to show pauses. Draw arrows above the words to show the intonation.

1. It makes me feel calm, | and powerful, | and intelligent.

2. I've already listed the primary colors: blue, red, and yellow.

3. We want to be healthy, to look good, to feel good about ourselves, and to feel important.

4. The first is blue, used by 33% of the top brands, second is red, used by 29%, and yellow is the third at 13%.

5. Out of all the money put towards online advertising, the most was spent in North America, followed by Western Europe, and then Asia.

B. With a partner, say the sentences in Apply, activity A with the appropriate pausing and intonation. Check your partner's pausing and intonation.

C. With a partner, pick five different categories of items you can buy (food, clothing, electronics, etc.). Make a list of at least three items in each category. Tell your partner the items you thought of. Use appropriate pausing and intonation.

> A: *Lisa, what items did you think of for "food"?*
>
> B: *I thought of <u>sandwiches</u>, | <u>pizza</u>, | and <u>salad</u>.*
>
> A: *You should pause more after the first item, and you need rising intonation there as well: <u>sandwiches</u>, | <u>pizza</u>, | and <u>salad</u>.*
>
> B: *Thank you, Miguel!*

End of Unit Task

In this unit, you learned how to understand ordinal numbers and percentages. You also learned how to use statistics when giving a speech. Review these skills by listening to a report about a fast-food restaurant and preparing a short presentation on one of your favorite products.

A. Go online to listen to the student's report on her class survey about Burger Supreme, a fast-food restaurant. Write the percentages you hear on the correct line.

| HOW OFTEN? | FAVORITE ITEM? | PRIMARY REASON? |

B. Work in a small group. Write four questions to ask about any product or company. Use *yes / no* or multiple-choice questions.

> 1. *What is your favorite brand of running shoes?*
>
> A. *Nike*
>
> B. *Adidas*
>
> C. *Puma*
>
> D. *Other:* _____

C. Work on your own now. Ask ten people in your class the four questions that your group wrote. If you wrote a multiple-choice question, use correct rising and falling intonation as you list the answers. Write the answers down as percentages.

D. Work with your group again. Report on the answers you got. Use percentages, fractions, and other expressions of quantity from the chart. Take notes on your classmates' reports.

Numbers	Percentages	Fractions	Other expressions of quantity
Two hundred and fifty (250)	Ninety percent (90%)	Nine tenths (9/10)	Nearly all
Five thousand (5,000)	Seventy-five percent (75%)	Three quarters (3/4)	Most
Three and a half billion (3,500,000,000)	Fifty percent (50%)	Half (1/2)	More than half Less than half
Six point five million (6,500,000)	Thirty-three percent (33%)	One-third (1/3)	About a quarter

Fifty percent (50%) like McDonalds. OR Half of the students like McDonalds.

E. Create a pie chart or bar graph to show your results.

Self-Assessment		
Yes	**No**	
☐	☐	I successfully understood ordinal numbers and percentages.
☐	☐	I conducted a short survey.
☐	☐	I used statistics in a short presentation.
☐	☐	I can use correct pausing and rising and falling intonation when listing items in a series.
☐	☐	I can correctly use the target vocabulary words from the unit.

Discussion Questions

With a partner or in a small group, discuss the following questions.

1. Does advertising and marketing work?

2. Are there good reasons to prevent some companies from advertising?

3. What makes an effective advertisement?

4

The Way We Communicate

In this unit, you will

> learn about social networking.
> understand what your online profile says about you.
> increase your understanding of the target academic words for this unit.

LISTENING AND SPEAKING SKILLS

> Organizing Facts and Opinions
> Expressing Opinions
> **PRONUNCIATION** Pronouncing the Letter *t*

Self-Assessment

Think about how well you know each target word, and check (✓) the appropriate column. I have...

TARGET WORDS	never seen this word before.	heard or seen the word but am not sure what it means.	seen or heard the word and understand what it means.	used the word confidently in *either* speaking or writing.
AWL				
🔑 comment				
🔑 community				
🔑 conduct				
🔑 contact				
🔑 locate				
🔑 respond				
🔑 select				
🔑 trend				

🔑 Oxford 3000™ keywords

Vocabulary Activities

A. Circle the word or phrase in parentheses that has the same meaning as the underlined word in the sentence. Compare your answers with a partner.

1. Social networks can build a sense of <u>community</u> (*loneliness* / *sharing* / *happiness*) for people who live far apart.

2. Most social networks allow users to make a <u>comment</u> (*opinion* / *argument* / *plan*) on someone's post.

3. Sometimes users ask questions and other people <u>respond</u> (*stay quiet* / *move on* / *answer*).

4. Many people like to use social media to <u>locate</u> (*find* / *text-message* / *make*) old friends.

5. If you don't like someone's <u>response</u> (*reaction* / *question* / *photos*), you can delete it.

6. I live in a pretty small <u>community</u> (*house* / *country* / *neighborhood*), so I enjoy using social networks as a way to meet new people.

The noun *community* means "all the people who live in a particular area, country, etc."

*The **community** was hit very hard by the tornado.*

It can also mean "a group of people who share the same religion, race, or job."

*The British **community** in Singapore is quite large.*

Community can also mean "the feeling of sharing things and belonging to a group in the place where you live."

*I feel a sense of **community** with the people in my class.*

CORPUS

B. Check (✓) the things you think make a *community*. With a partner, discuss your ideas.

____ a class

____ a hive of bees

____ an apartment building

____ a sports team

____ passengers on a train

____ shoppers at a mall

C. The noun *location* means the place or position of something. With a partner, match the item on the left with its usual location on the right.

_d_ 1. pens   a. bathroom cabinet

____ 2. car   b. refrigerator

____ 3. cell phone   c. pocket

____ 4. milk   d. desk

____ 5. medicine   e. recycling bin

____ 6. plastic bottle   f. parking lot

D. Read the pairs of sentences below. Which one do you think is the first comment? Which one is the response? Write C (comment) or R (response). Then compare your answers with a partner.

_C_ 1. It's a beautiful day today.

_R_   I agree. Let's go for a run.

____ 2. That's not too much.

____   My friend spends only one hour a day online.

____ 3. Children under 16 years of age shouldn't use social networks.

____   How can we keep them offline?

____ 4. Really? I find that surprising.

____   Most teenagers are online every day.

____ 5. I've never used it. I don't want to communicate with a lot of people at once.

____   Twitter is a good way to stay in touch with many people at once.

____ 6. More people get their news from social media these days than from regular newspapers.

____   That's understandable. They can read news online anytime they want.

____ 7. But you have to be careful about the kind of pictures you post.

____   Social networking sites are a good way to share photos.

About the Topic

People today spend a lot of time online. They are on their computers, smartphones, and tablets. They often connect with others through social media. Social media refers to social networks such as Twitter, Google+, and Pinterest.

Before You Listen

Read these questions. Discuss your answers in a small group.

1. Who do you talk to every day? How do you communicate?
2. What social networks do you know about?
3. How do you think social networks affect your relationships?

Listen

Read the Listen for Main Ideas activity below. Go online to listen to an interview about social networking and the different opinions people have about it. How does social networking affect friendships?

Listen for Main Ideas

Mark each sentence as *T* (true) or *F* (false). Work with a partner. Restate false sentences to make them correct.

__T__ 1. The discussion is mostly about young people's use of social networks.

____ 2. Both guests are parents and researchers.

____ 3. Social media can make people feel anxious.

____ 4. Employers might look at job applicants' online profiles.

____ 5. Social media is not good for new college students.

____ 6. Henry and Jane have different opinions about social media use.

NOTE-TAKING SKILL   Organizing Facts and Opinions

LEARN

A fact is something that is true. A fact can be proved.

Nelson Mandela was president of South Africa.

Brasilia is the capital of Brazil.

An opinion is someone's feelings or thoughts about something. Here are some phrases used to express an opinion:

I believe social networking is improving communication among young people.

You should follow the instructions to get the best results.

Words and phrases used to express opinions:

     modals: should, shouldn't, must,

     adjectives: beautiful, favorite, stronger, better

     phrases: I believe, I think, In my opinion

When listening, you can organize facts and opinions with a T-chart.

APPLY

A. Read the statements Jane makes in the radio program. Write the letters of the statements under *Fact* or *Opinion* in the T-chart.

a. I think social media helps more than it hurts.

b. Both my children are older teens, and one has just started college.

c. I believe they are pretty smart about what they put online.

d. I just think social media networks are a way to make plans and communicate with friends far away.

e. I saw a survey which found that 37% of companies look at job applicants' online profiles.

Fact	Opinion
	a

Read the statements below and place them in the correct side of the T-chart: *Fact* or *Opinion*.

social media helps more than it hurts

employers look at social networks

37% of companies look at job applicants' online profiles

people who used social media spent more time each day with offline friends than people who didn't use social media

more friends online did not mean better relationships

social networks can help kids who have just started college

social networks are a way to make plans and communicate with friends far away

Fact	Opinion

B. Go online to listen to the radio program again. Who gave each fact and opinion? Write *J* for Jane or *H* for Henry next to each point. Add other facts or opinions you hear.

C. Read the information you wrote in the T-chart. Discuss with a partner. What is your opinion?

Vocabulary Activities

A. For each sentence, cross out the word or phrase in parentheses that has a different meaning. Use a dictionary to help. Compare answers with a partner.

1. Some people don't know how to (*conduct themselves / behave / act / ~~contact~~*) online. They don't follow basic rules.

2. It's important to (*choose / select / locate / pick*) the right photo—the one that shows you at your best.

3. You want someone's (*trend / response / reaction / answer*) to your post to be positive.

4. I don't put my phone number on a profile. If someone wants to (*respond to / comment on / identify with / react to*) something I post, they can email me through the social networking site.

5. One recent online (*change / community / trend / tendency*) is to list your location at the moment.

B. When you *select* something, you choose it or decide that you want it. Check (✓) the things you think about when you select a school. Then share your ideas with a partner. Which one is the most important to you?

____ location ____ cost ____ courses of study ____ weather

____ friends ____ size ____ teachers ____ library

C. Some of the target words have multiple meanings. For the target words below, match the dictionary definitions on the left with the example sentences on the right. Check your answers with a partner.

conduct (noun, verb)

Definitions

b 1. to do a particular activity

___ 2. to direct a group of people who are singing or playing music

___ 3. to behave or act in a particular way

___ 4. to lead someone around a place

___ 5. to allow heat or electricity to pass

___ 6. a person's behavior in a situation

Example Sentences

a. He conducted himself poorly.

b. They conducted the experiment last year.

c. Your conduct online may affect your employment.

d. The concert was conducted by Olaf Gregg.

e. The tour guide conducted us around the museum.

f. Water conducts electricity, so don't drop your hair dryer in the bathtub.

contact (noun, verb)

Definitions

____ 1. to communicate with somebody

____ 2. the act of communicating with somebody

____ 3. the state of touching something

____ 4. the state of meeting somebody or having to deal with something

____ 5. a person you know who can help you

____ 6. an electrical connection

Example Sentences

a. His fingers came into contact with the ball.

b. She contacted me by phone.

c. Do you have any contacts in media? I'm looking for a job.

d. As a judge, she often has contact with lawyers.

e. The wires have to touch both contacts or the battery won't work.

f. I don't have much contact with John anymore.

D. The verb *contact* means to communicate with someone. With a partner, discuss how you contact the people in the situations below. For example, you may contact them by email, text message, phone call, letter, or in person.

1. your teacher about missing a class
2. your mother about her birthday present
3. your friend about meeting for lunch
4. your boss about changing your schedule
5. a store about a defective camera you bought
6. your teammates about a soccer practice

About the Topic

Most colleges and universities have a career center. A career center is a place where students can go to get advice about finding a job after college. The career center often gives talks on topics such as writing a resume, interviewing for a job, and behaving professionally.

Before You Listen

Discuss these questions with a partner.

1. If you have an online profile, how do you decide what to post on it?

2. How are online identities different from real-life ones?

3. Who do you think looks at your online profile?

Listen

Read the Listen for Main Ideas exercise below. Go online to listen to a counselor give a short talk called "What Your Profile Says about You." Your profile is a description of yourself. A job / employee profile includes information about your work and educational experience. A personal profile may list your interests and activities.

Listen for Main Ideas

Listen to the audio and answer the questions. Compare your answers with a partner.

1. Who is the counselor speaking to?

   _____

2. Why is she talking about this subject?

   _____

3. What does she think is most important in a profile?

   _____

4. What kind of photo is a good one to use?

   _____

5. What kind of information should people post online?

   _____

SPEAKING SKILL　Expressing Opinions

LEARN

Expressing opinions in an appropriate way shows you are following the topic and have given it some thought. You can use these expressions to give your opinions as you listen to others.

I think …　　　　　　　　*In my opinion, …*

I feel …　　　　　　　　*I believe …*

If you ask me, …　　　　　*In my view, …*

You can also use similar phrases to explain another person's opinion: *In the writer's opinion, the writer thinks …*

APPLY

A. Go online to listen to the audio again. Complete the statements. Write the phrases you hear that introduce opinions.

1. _____*In my opinion*_____ , the most important thing is photos.

2. _____ that it's a good idea to show something about your personality or interests in the photo.

3. _____ that was very interesting.

4. _____ that a profile should show your personality and your good points.

5. _____ , even the little things are important.

B. Work with a partner. Give your opinion on each topic. Introduce your opinion with one of the expressions in activity A.

1. Why is it important to be careful about what you post online?

2. How much time do you think a college student should spend on social networking sites each day? Why?

3. Do you think online friendships are as important as real-life ones? Why or why not?

C. Choose one of the questions in activity B. Prepare to give your opinion on that topic. Work with a new partner. Take turns presenting your topics. Express your opinions using the expressions in activity A.

PRONUNCIATION SKILL · Pronouncing the Letter *t*

LEARN

The letter *t* can be pronounced in different ways depending on the sounds that come before and after it.

A. When the letter *t* is the final letter of a word and the following word starts with a consonant, the /t/ is often dropped. Go online to listen.

1. just started
2. post the

B. When the letter *t* is the final letter of a word and the following word starts with the letter *y*, the t and y are pronounced as the /ch/ sound. These words are most commonly *you*, *your*, and *you're*. Go online to listen.

/ch/

"What Your Profile Says About You"

C. When the letter *t* is the final letter of a word and it follows a vowel, it often is not released. The speaker holds his / her breath. Go online to listen.

1. at this
2. out there
3. important topic

APPLY

A. Go online to listen to the following phrases. Draw a slash through a deleted sound. Repeat each phrase using correct pronunciation.

1. Some studies suggest that people who have a lot of online friends also have a lot of offline friends.
2. Most people find social media relaxing.
3. And they used them in the way Jane just mentioned.
4. One has just started at college.

B. Go online to listen to the following sentences. Draw a circle connecting the final *t* and the initial *y*. Write /ch/ above the circle. Repeat each phrase using the /ch/ sound.

/ch/

1. It is important that you conduct yourself in a polite manner online as well as in person.
2. I believe that it's a good idea to show something about your personality or interests in the photo.
3. After all, what you post online says a lot about you.

C. With a partner, ask each other's opinions about social networking. Use the sentence starter "Tell me what you think about … ." Use the /ch/ sound to connect *what* and *you*. Use deleted and unreleased /t/ sounds.

> *A: Tell me what you think about posting your resume online, Angela.*
>
> *B: I just posted my resume on a site. I like to have my information out there.*

End of Unit Task

In this unit you learned how to listen for facts and opinions. You also learned about expressing facts and opinions. Review these skills by discussing your opinions about these topics. Listen to other students express their opinions and see what facts they give to support what they say.

A. Look at the photos on a social media site. Do you think these are good photos to post? Why or why not? Discuss your ideas with a partner. Talk about your own social media use. How often do you go online? How often do you post or comment?

B. As you listen to your partner, write the facts and opinions you hear in the T-chart.

Fact	Opinion

C. With a partner, choose one of the topics below. What is your opinion? Try to add facts to support your opinion. You may have to do some research.

- Should profile photos be beautiful?
- Should you try to have as many online friends as possible?
- Should you say a lot online?
- Are there more good things about social media than bad?

D. Find a new partner. Present your ideas. Use expressions like the ones below to show your opinions. Where possible, use facts to support your opinions.

| I think ... | I believe ... | I feel ... |
| In my opinion, ... | In my view, ... | If you ask me, ... |

E. Share your ideas with the class. What do most of the students think about these topics?

		Self-Assessment
Yes	**No**	
☐	☐	I successfully organized facts and opinions in a T-chart.
☐	☐	I successfully expressed my opinion on a topic.
☐	☐	I tried to use facts to support my opinions.
☐	☐	I can pronounce the letter *t* in connected speech.
☐	☐	I can correctly use the target vocabulary words from the unit.

Discussion Questions

With a partner or in a small group, discuss the following questions.

1. What are the benefits of social media?
2. What are the problems with social media?
3. Can social media help someone find a job?

UNIT 5

The Games We Play

In this unit, you will

> learn about the importance of playtime for children's development.
> learn what makes a workplace creative and innovative.
> increase your understanding of the target academic words for this unit.

LISTENING AND SPEAKING SKILLS

> Listening for Main Ideas
> Using Examples to Support Main Ideas
> **PRONUNCIATION** Adverbial Phrases

Self-Assessment

Think about how well you know each target word, and check (✓) the appropriate column. I have...

TARGET WORDS	never seen this word before.	heard or seen the word but am not sure what it means.	heard or seen the word and understand what it means.	used the word confidently in *either* speaking or writing.
AWL				
🔑 colleague				
🔑 concentrate				
🔑 convince				
🔑 emphasis				
🔑 generate				
🔑 schedule				
🔑 similar				
🔑 theme				

🔑 Oxford 3000™ keywords

Vocabulary Activities

A. Complete the paragraph with the target words from the box below.

concentrate	convince	emphasize	theme

Parents today have a hard job. They want to help their children learn,

but it's difficult to know the best way to help. For example, many parents

use technology, or a variety of electronics, to help children learn to read.

They buy educational video games for their very young children. These

games often ___emphasize___ letters and beginning reading skills, and they
                (1)

are fun. The problem is that if you play video games to learn to read, it

is harder to _____ when you read a real book. It can be hard to
               (2)

_____ children to read real books. The computer games seem a lot
    (3)

more fun than reading a book. The other problem is that when children

are on the computer, they are not outside in nature. They don't get fresh air

and exercise. There are risks with technology—our children might become

deficient in, or without, social skills and in the understanding of the natural

world. I guess my _____ in this post is this: Technology is only one
                      (4)

tool for teaching children. It shouldn't be the only tool.

B. Complete the Word Form Chart on page 51 with the correct forms of the target words. Use a dictionary to check your answers.

concentrate	convince	de-emphasize	emphatic	theme
concentrated	convinced	emphasis	emphatically	unconvinced
concentration	convincing	emphasize	thematic	unconvincing

Word Form Chart			
Noun	**Verb**	**Adjective**	**Adverb**
concentration			

C. Use the correct form of *emphasis* to complete the sentences below. Compare answers with a partner.

1. "Absolutely not," my mother said __emphatically__ . "You cannot go out tonight."

2. I think there is too much _____ placed on grades and not enough on learning.

3. The president _____ the ways that the law could help.

4. The student was _____ about the danger of global warming in his presentation to the class.

D. For each of the following, write one thing that will convince you it is true. Then share your ideas with a partner.

1. social networks help relationships *I found my best friend from childhood through a social network.*

2. people are basically good _____

3. you are really smart _____

4. you are ready for a test _____

The noun *theme* means "a subject or main idea in a talk, piece of writing, or art."

> *The speaker addressed the **theme** of the importance of play in her talk last night.*

It can also refer to a piece of music that is repeated, especially in a movie.

> *At the fireworks display last night, the orchestra played the **theme** from Star Wars.*

CORPUS

E. Complete the sentences with your ideas.

1. For a party with a holiday theme, we should have …
2. The theme of this unit is …
3. Hip-hop music often includes themes of …
4. I think boys and men like movies with themes of …

About the Topic

Children play outside less now than they did 50 years ago. One reason is that schools often don't give children time to play. Another reason is that families are very busy. Parents often work and the children go to after-school activities.

Before You Watch

Read these questions. Discuss your answers in a small group.

1. How do most children spend their free time?

2. Do you think it is important for children to have a lot of time to play? Why or why not?

3. How has play changed in the last 30 years?

Watch

Read the Listen for Main Ideas activity below. Go online to watch the video about a children's camp with a nature theme.

Listen for Main Ideas

Check (✓) the ideas mentioned in the video.

____ 1. The children live in the city and need to see nature.

_✓_ 2. The children enjoy spending time outdoors.

____ 3. Parents think their children spend too much time on electronics.

____ 4. It's important for kids to meet other children from different places.

____ 5. Richard Louv thinks nature helps children to learn.

____ 6. Children can get better at art.

____ 7. The children can see animals.

NOTE-TAKING SKILL Listening for Main Ideas

LEARN

When you are listening to a presentation or lecture, it is important to understand the main idea the speaker is trying to get across.

Speakers will often identify the main ideas of their speech by stating them at the beginning and end of their presentation.

Signaling the main idea	
The main thing is ...	*The important thing is ...*
What I want you to understand is ...	*The most important thing to know is ...*

Sometimes a speaker uses repetition, including the use of synonyms, or words that are about the same topic.

APPLY

A. Watch the video again. Check (✓) the words or ideas you hear.

✓ plant	___ iPod Touch	___ outdoors
___ food	___ art	___ walking
___ TV	___ nature	___ high tech
___ movies	___ technology	___ animals
___ pond	___ sports	___ playing
___ mud	___ outside	___ screen
___ electronics		

B. Work with a partner. Complete the diagram below. Write the two main ideas you and your partner heard. Then write the words you checked in activity A in the circle with its main idea.

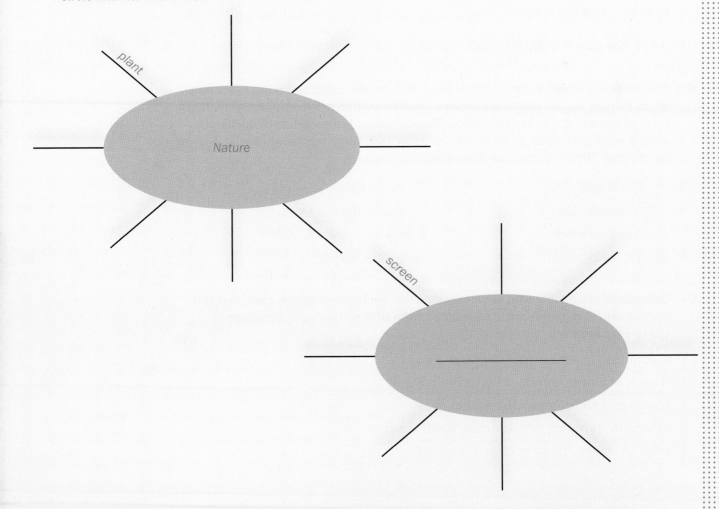

SPEAKING

Vocabulary Activities

A. Complete the paragraph with the correct forms of the target words in the box below.

generate	schedule	colleague	theme	similar	concentrate

Many companies that work with social networks or other technology have

___similar___ work environments. Because they are all about _____
   (1)   (2)

ideas, these companies want their workers to be happy. Usually, the work

environment is open, that is there are no offices with walls, and everyone has

about the same amount of workspace. Even though the space is open, people

have to _____ on their work. _____ can meet often to discuss
        (3)   (4)

projects. Like Google, these companies offer free laundry and free food. The

workers often don't follow set _____. They come and go at different
                                 (5)

times, but they usually stay late. The _____ is fun and creativity!
                                             (6)

B. A *schedule* is a plan or list of times when things will happen or a list that shows when planes, buses, and other forms of transportation arrive and leave a place. Look at each of the schedules below. Do you check the schedule everyday (D), once a week (W), once a month (M), or never (N)? Write the letter of your answer on the line. Then discuss your answers with a partner.

____ bus schedule   ____ calendar on your phone

____ train schedule   ____ movie theater listings

____ flight schedule   ____ sports team schedule

____ TV listings   ____ gym schedule

C. *Colleagues* are people who work together. For each group below, cross out the person who is probably not a colleague of the others. Use your dictionary to check your answers.

1. teacher, lab assistant, librarian, ~~bus driver~~

2. doctor, engineer, nurse, physician's assistant

3. cook, server, customer, dishwasher

4. salesclerk, reporter, news anchor, weatherperson

5. pilot, professor, flight attendant, co-pilot

The adjective *similar* means "like someone or something but not exactly the same." *Similarly* is the adverb form.

> *My sister and I have **similar** interests—she likes to play the piano, and I like to play the guitar.*

> *The two schools are **similar** in that they both offer strong science courses.*

> *The two men were **similarly** successful in their careers.*

The noun is *similarity*.

> *There are many **similarities** between the two software companies.*

CORPUS

D. Cross out the word or idea that is not similar to the others. Explain your answer to a partner.

1. soccer, volleyball, basketball, ~~yoga~~

   You need a ball to play soccer, volleyball, and basketball, but not to do yoga.

2. biology, art, history, math
3. breakfast, eat, drink, cook
4. Morocco, Tunisia, Italy, Algeria
5. brother, sister, niece, neighbor
6. kind, friendly, mean, generous
7. similarity, theme, concentrate, emphasis

About the Topic

People spend a lot of time at work. Companies that focus on developing new ideas, often want to create a more fun, open, and different kind of work environment. In addition to this, if the company offers good benefits to employees, they can attract talented people to the job.

Before You Listen

Read these questions. Discuss your answers in a small group.

1. What are some ways that companies try to keep their workers happy?

2. What is your idea of a good place to work?

3. Have you heard of the company Google? What kind of people do you think work there?

Listen

Read the Listen for Main Ideas below.
Go online to listen to a report that describes Google's work environment. Would you like to work here?

Listen for Main Ideas

Read the questions about the report. Work with a partner to ask and answer the questions.

1. How are technology companies different from other businesses?

2. How does the company want employees to feel?

3. Why is food important to the workers?

4. What healthy activities can employees do at work?

5. How does Google keep its employees at work for a long time every day?

PRESENTATION SKILL | Using Examples to Support Main Ideas

LEARN

When you give a presentation, you need a clear main idea.

Once you have chosen your main idea and examples to support it, use the phrases below to introduce those examples.

For example, ...	*For instance, ...*	*like ...*
One way that ... is	*Another way that ... is*	*such as ...*

APPLY

A. Listen to the report on Google again. What are the three main ways that Google tries to make its employees happy? Complete the main points in the outline below.

1. *First main point:*
   Examples: by feeding them.

2. *Second main point:*
   Examples:

3. *Third main point:*
   Examples:

B. The speaker gives examples to support each main idea. Go online to listen again, and complete the examples for each main point in the outline.

C. Work with a partner. For each main idea below, give at least two examples to support it.

- It is important for children to have time outside to play.
- Workplaces should provide benefits to attract better workers.
- Students need to manage their time well to succeed in school.

D. Prepare a three-minute presentation with your partner.

1. Choose your main idea. Use one of the topics from activity C above, or your own idea.
2. Provide examples to support your idea.
3. Present your idea to another group. Then switch roles.
4. Listen to the other group's presentation and take notes on the main ideas and examples. Then confirm with the speaker that you understood the main idea and examples.

PRONUNCIATION SKILL   Adverbial Phrases

LEARN

A. Adverbial phrases are phrases that begin with an adverb such as *after*, *while*, or *when*. When an adverbial phrase is at the beginning of a sentence, insert a pause after the phrase. Go online to listen.

1. If the employees have everything they need at work, | they won't have to leave.

2. And with a good breakfast, | workers can concentrate on their work.

B. Adverbial phrases use rising intonation and are followed by falling intonation at the end of a sentence. Go online to listen to the sentences. Notice the intonation.

1. Before the end of the day, | employees have another great meal.

2. Because there is no set schedule, | workers can take a break whenever they want.

APPLY

A. Insert a line to show the pause and draw a line of rising intonation. Go online to listen. Check your answers.

1. After lunch, | it's back to work for several hours.
2. About once a week, workers play volleyball in the late afternoon.
3. Before staff leave for home, they can pick up their laundry.
4. In the morning, staff can drop off their children at the daycare center.
5. After arriving at work, they can have a free breakfast in one of the dining rooms at Google.

B. Say the sentences from Apply, activity A above. Focus on pausing and intonation.

C. With a partner, talk about your schedule. Describe when you complete your household duties, family responsibilities, and school work. Use adverbial phrases. Make sure to use appropriate pauses and intonation.

When I …	Before I …
Once I …	After I …
After breakfast / lunch / dinner, …	At 8 / 9 / 10 p.m., …
In the morning / afternoon / evening, …	When it's time to …

A: When I get home from school, | I make dinner right away.

B: After that, | do you spend time with your family?

End of Unit Task

In this unit, you learned how to listen for main ideas and how to use examples to support main ideas. To review, you will listen for main ideas and supporting examples as you listen to a presentation. Then you will prepare a short presentation using examples to support your main ideas.

A. Do video games give children the same skills as sports? Why or why not? Discuss your ideas with a partner.

B. Listen to the presentation on the benefits of video games. Take notes on the main ideas and supporting examples.

1. First main point: _____

   Example(s): _____

   _____

2. Second main point: _____

   Example(s): _____

   _____

3. Third main point: _____

   Example(s): _____

   _____

C. Work in groups of three. Take turns retelling a main idea from the presentation and giving examples to support it.

D. Choose one of the topics below. Prepare a two-minute presentation on the topic. Use the outline that follows.

playtime during the school day	the best way to use technology in class
the perfect work environment	activities that help students learn
the best way to generate new ideas	benefits of organized sports

1. First main point: _____

    Example(s): _____

    _____

2. Second main point: _____

    Example(s): _____

    _____

3. Third main point: _____

    Example(s): _____

    _____

Self-Assessment		
Yes	**No**	
☐	☐	I successfully took notes on main ideas.
☐	☐	I successfully took notes on supporting examples.
☐	☐	I used examples to support my main ideas in a presentation.
☐	☐	I can use correct intonation and pausing with adverbial phrases.
☐	☐	I can correctly use the target vocabulary words from the unit.

Discussion Questions

With a partner or in a small group, discuss the following questions.

1. Why is it important for children to play outside?
2. Is it important for adults to "play"?
3. What can families do to make sure children have enough time to play?

Adaptations

In this unit, you will

> learn about the effects of bringing animals from one place to another.

> understand how farming methods create new types of plants.

> increase your understanding of the target academic words for this unit.

LISTENING AND SPEAKING SKILLS

> Creating a Timeline

> Sequence Words and Phrases

> **PRONUNCIATION** Linking Sounds

Self-Assessment

Think about how well you know each target word, and check (✓) the appropriate column. I have...

TARGET WORDS	never seen this word before.	heard or seen the word but am not sure what it means.	heard or seen the word and understand what it means.	used the word confidently in *either* speaking or writing.
AWL				
🔑 challenge				
🔑 eliminate				
guideline				
🔑 institute				
instruct				
modify				
🔑 secure				
sequence				
🔑 specific				
🔑 transfer				

🔑 Oxford 3000™ keywords

Vocabulary Activities

A. Complete the paragraph with the target words in the box below.

secure	transfer	specific	sequence	guidelines

Many countries have ___guidelines___ about bringing animals in from other
(1)

places. These countries want to keep the local wildlife _____ from
(2)

the diseases that new animals can carry. For example, travelers often must

follow a _____ of steps to bring in a new pet. They must prove that
(3)

the animal has taken medicine to protect it from _____ illnesses.
(4)

Sometimes the animal also has to live alone for a few weeks before the

government will _____ it into the country.
(5)

B. *Guidelines* are official rules or advice that tell you how to do something. With
a partner, discuss what types of guidelines you might find in each of the
following situations.

1. returning a purchase to a store
2. registering for a marathon
3. planning a celebration
4. packing for a flight
5. preparing a short presentation

C. *Secure* is an adjective with several meanings. With a partner, match each
definition to the correct sentences.

a. not worried
b. safe
c. locked or protected

___c__ 1. The door isn't very secure. I think I can open it.

____ 2. Are you feeling secure about your job? I hear your company is firing some
people.

____ 3. Don't climb on that ladder. It's not very secure.

____ 4. Many hotels offer a safe in your room so you can keep your things secure.

____ 5. She feels very secure about taking the test tomorrow.

____ 6. The railing next to the stairs isn't very secure.

D. *Specific* means "exact" or "clear." It is the opposite of *general*. Work with a partner to decide if each example is specific (**S**) or general (**G**). Restate any general statements to make them more specific using your own ideas.

_G_ 1. Go a few miles. Turn toward the river when you reach downtown.

  Go straight for 3.1 miles. Then turn left at the light onto Irving Street.

___ 2. My favorite kind of ice cream is vanilla.

___ 3. Greta is left-handed. Her mother is also left-handed.

___ 4. Some things run in families.

___ 5. I like desserts.

___ 6. Go 2.4 miles. Turn right on High Street.

___ 7. Some animals are friendly.

E. Complete the sequences with the next logical item.

1. January, February, March, _____*April*_____

2. Ant, Bird, Cat, Dog, _____

3. 65, 70, 75, _____

4. Thursday, Friday, Saturday, _____

5. English 1, English 2, English 3, _____

F. Complete the statements about the sequences above. Use words from the box below to show the relationship.

day	month	alphabetical	numerical	college course

1. Number 3 shows a(n) _____*numerical*_____ sequence.

2. Number 1 shows a(n) _____ sequence.

3. Number 5 shows a(n) _____ sequence.

4. Number 2 shows a(n) _____ sequence.

5. Number 4 shows a(n) _____ sequence.

About the Topic

Humans have been bringing animals from one place to another for hundreds of years. Some of these animals are very successful in their new environments. None of the other animals there can eat it, and none of the smaller animals or plants in the new place can protect themselves against it. This means that the new animal has a lot of food to eat, and faces very little danger. Soon there is a large population of the new animal in the new place.

Before You Listen

Read these questions. Discuss your answers in a small group.

1. What natural environment do you think has the most interesting wildlife?

2. What plants and animals do you see every day?

3. Do you know about any local wildlife that was actually brought from another place?

Listen

Read the Listen for Main Ideas activity below. Go online to listen to a lecture about an animal in a new environment.

Listen for Main Ideas

Mark each sentence as *T* (true) or *F* (false). Work with a partner. Restate false sentences to make them correct.

_T_ 1. The speaker is lecturing about a type of toad that was brought to Australia.

____ 2. An *adaptation* is a change in a plant or animal's body or behavior because of a change in its environment.

____ 3. Scientists thought that the cane toads would eat sugar cane plants.

____ 4. Some Australian snakes developed longer bodies because of cane toads.

____ 5. Cane toads are moving west through Australia faster now than they were 50 years ago.

NOTE-TAKING SKILL   Creating a Timeline

LEARN

A timeline is a good way to organize the events of a narrative, for example, the life of Jane Goodall, the English scientist:

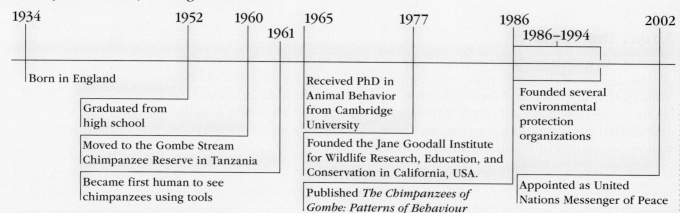

1934 ... 1952 ... 1960 ... 1961 ... 1965 ... 1977 ... 1986 ... 1986–1994 ... 2002

Born in England

Graduated from high school

Moved to the Gombe Stream Chimpanzee Reserve in Tanzania

Became first human to see chimpanzees using tools

Received PhD in Animal Behavior from Cambridge University

Founded the Jane Goodall Institute for Wildlife Research, Education, and Conservation in California, USA.

Published *The Chimpanzees of Gombe: Patterns of Behaviour*

Founded several environmental protection organizations

Appointed as United Nations Messenger of Peace

Think about the most important events in your life. On the timeline below, write the events above the line and the corresponding dates below the line.

Born in _____

APPLY

 A. Go online to listen to the lecture again. Put the events in time order along the timeline. Add other dates and notes. Abbreviate the notes so they will fit.

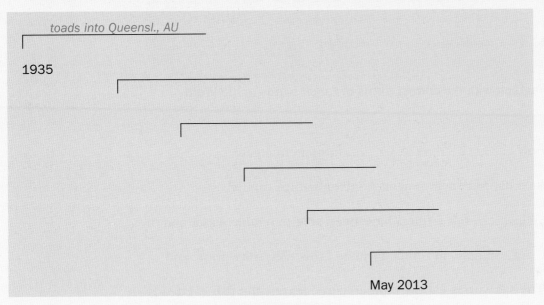

- Cane toads enter Northern Territory, Australia
- Phillips finds snakes in Queensland have smaller heads than other Australian snakes
- Western Australian government publishes Cane Toad App for smartphones
- Phillips finds cane toads moving west have longer legs than original cane toads
- Pemberton brings cane toads to Queensland, Australia
- Cane toads enter Kimberley, Western Australia

B. Work with a partner. Use your timeline and notes. Take turns retelling the events.

Vocabulary Activities

Word Form Chart			
Noun	**Verb**	**Adjective**	**adverb**
challenge	challenge	challenging	_____
elimination	eliminate	eliminated	_____
institution	institute	instituted institutional	institutionally
instructor	instruct	instructive	instructively
modification	modify	modified	_____

A. Complete the paragraph with the correct forms of target words in the Word Form Chart.

Some scientists now _____*instruct*_____ farmers to create
 (1. teach)

farms that are like a natural environment. Copying nature can be

_____, but farmers have been able to reduce waste and
 (2. new or difficult)

earn more profit. For example, in China, farmers grow fish, silkworms, and

mulberry trees. The silkworms eat the mulberry tree leaves, the fish eat dead

silkworms, and mud from the fish pond helps the trees grow. Farmers there

have _____ many of the chemicals used to help crops
 (3. removed something not wanted)

grow. With governments beginning to _____ limits on
 (4. put into place a new system)

chemicals, more farmers may make _____ like these
 (5. small changes)

to their farms.

B. Write each synonym below the correct target word in the chart.

| hard | teacher | changed | different | difficult | rule |
| advice | remove | erase | cut out | demanding | instruction |

challenging	instructor	modified	eliminate	guideline
hard				

The verb *instruct* means to teach someone something or to tell someone what he / she must do.

*The teacher **instructed** the students to use a pencil on the test.*

It is similar to *teach*, but *instruct* is followed by people (for example, *students*), or by a phrase (for example, *in using the computer*).

*The lab assistant **instructed** the students in using the computer.*

You can use *teach* by itself (He teaches.) It can also be followed by a school subject or by people (English, children).

*He **taught** in Saudi Arabia.*

*I **teach** English.*

*She **teaches** children.*

CORPUS

C. Write the target word from the box below that works best with the phrases below. Add one phrase for each question.

| challenge | eliminate | instruct | modify |

1. ___challenge___ authority, a speeding ticket, my beliefs, ___the students___

2. _____ a diet, the exercise, plans, _____

3. _____ ESL students, in college writing, _____

4. _____ jobs, suspects, crime, _____

D. Work with a partner. Discuss the following.

1. Should we eliminate or modify our use of electricity? Why?
2. Should we modify or eliminate very large cars, such as SUVs? Why?
3. Should Internet use be modified or eliminated in young teenagers?
4. Should we modify or eliminate large, modern farms? Why?

About the Topic

To feed the world's increasing population, some farmers have begun growing food using seeds that have been modified in laboratories. They want to produce more crops using fewer harmful chemicals. This has been successful in some cases. Planting crops with these seeds has also had unintended consequences

Before You Listen

Read these questions. Discuss your answers in a small group.

1. Have you ever grown your own food?
2. How has farming in your region changed over the past few decades?
3. What do you think is the safest way to grow enough food for everyone?

Listen

Read the Listen for Main Ideas activity below. Go online to listen to the student presentation on modern farming and "superweeds." The student explains how unwanted plants can become stronger and harder to kill.

Listen for Main Ideas

Read the statements about the student's presentation. Work with a partner. Choose the word that best completes each statement.

1. Superweeds are **herbicides** / **plants** that are hard to kill.
2. Weeds can become **resistant** / **smaller** when farmers use only one method to fight them.
3. Some seeds are designed to **survive** / **produce** herbicides.
4. Farmers stopped **watering** / **plowing** their fields.
5. One way to fight superweeds is to plant a variety of **soils** / **crops**.

LEARN

In your classes, you will often have to describe an event, retell a story you heard or read, or explain a process. In conversation, you will have to tell about things that happened to you or to someone else. Using sequence words and phrases will help you. They show the order of events. Read the list of sequence words and phrases. Can you think of other words or phrases you could add to the list?

First, ...	Second, ...
Third, ...	Finally, ...
Next, ...	Then, ...
After that, ...	After she arrived, ...
	Before she left, ...

APPLY

A. Listen to the presentation again. What sequence words and phrases do you hear?

1. _____

2. _____

3. _____

4. _____

B. Put the sentences below in the correct order. Then retell the sequence of events to a partner.

____ 1. When most of the weeds die, the only ones left are the weeds that can resist the herbicide.

____ 2. Next, the farmer begins using only that herbicide to kill weeds.

____ 3. Then, almost all of the weeds in the field are eliminated.

____ 4. At the end, these weeds spread throughout the field and become superweeds.

____ 5. First, a farmer plants seeds that cannot be hurt by a specific herbicide.

C. Work with a partner. Take turns describing an event that you experienced, or explaining a process that you are familiar with. Take notes as your partner speaks. Then retell the events in sequence.

PRONUNCIATION SKILL   Linking Sounds

LEARN

When you speak, you often connect the final sound in one word to the initial sound in the following word.

A. When any consonant sound comes before a vowel sound, link the two sounds together. Go online to listen.

1. The guidelines on scientific research were not strict at that time.

2. This eliminates almost all of the weeds in Joe's field.

B. When a consonant sound comes before another consonant sound, link the two sounds together. Go online to listen.

1. Cane beetles were damaging the sugar plants there.

2. Some weeds were able to live after being dug up.

C. When the sound /p/, /b/, /t/, /d/, /k/, /g/, /ch/, or /dge/ links to the same sound, say the sound once, hold the position for the sound, pause slightly, and then say the next word. Go online to listen to the examples.

1. Animals that eat cane toads could die.

2. Superweeds have begun taking resources away from crop plants.

3. We will look at which changes farmers have made.

4. Regulating the movement of animals across country borders is a huge job.

APPLY

A. Say the example sentences in Learn, activities A, B, and C.

B. Make a list of what you do to stay healthy. Then note which final sounds link with the initial sounds of the word that follows it.

> I sleep eight hours every night.

C. With two partners, talk about what you wrote.

> A: To stay well, I eat fruits and vegetables for every snack.
> B: I walk around my neighborhood and drink orange juice at breakfast.

End of Unit Task

In this unit, you learned how to create a timeline to record events and dates and how to use sequence words and phrases to narrate events. To review, you will use a timeline to record events and dates as you listen to a report. Then you will practice retelling the events to a partner before you use sequence words and phrases to narrate your own series of events.

A. Listen to the report on the wolf population of Yellowstone Park in Montana, U.S. Take notes on a timeline using **1884** as the first date and **2013** as the last date.

Wolves in Yellowstone Park

2013 ———— U.S. Fish and Wildlife Service proposed removing wolves from Endangered Species list.

1800s ———— Wolves are common in Montana.

B. Work with a partner. Find the correct sequence of events. When did these things happen? Ask and answer questions.

_1930s_ Park employees begin to report changes in Yellowstone's animals, plants and streams.

_____ Montana creates a Wolf Bounty Law.

_____ A report in *Yellowstone Science* confirms that the ecosystem is becoming more healthy.

_____ 15 wolves are released in Yellowstone.

_____ Wolves are attacking farm animals.

_____ The U.S. federal puts wolves on the Endangered Species list.

C. Find a new partner. Take turns narrating the events of wolves being removed from and then brought back to Yellowstone National Park. Use sequence words and phrases.

D. Think about an event or series of events you know about. Use one of the ideas below or your own idea. Write the important events on the timeline.

an important historical event   an important event in your life

the events in a movie or book   the most exciting thing that happened to you

an embarrassing situation   a true story you heard

E. Using sequence words and phrases, narrate the event(s) to a partner.

Self-Assessment		
Yes	**No**	
☐	☐	I successfully took notes on a timeline.
☐	☐	I successfully retold a historical event using sequence words and phrases.
☐	☐	I used sequence words and phrases to narrate an event or series of events.
☐	☐	I can use linking sounds when I speak.
☐	☐	I can correctly use the target vocabulary words from the unit.

Discussion Questions

With a partner or in a small group, discuss the following questions.

1. Wild animals can harm farm animals or pets. Should humans be allowed to hurt wild animals to protect livestock or pets?

2. What measures can a city or country take to keep wild animals safe?

3. Why does removing one animal cause so many changes in an ecosystem?

4. Should people be allowed to visit nature preserves, or should the land be left untouched by humans?

Patenting Our Lives

In this unit, you will

> learn about patents, copyrights, and intellectual property.
> increase your understanding of the target academic words in this unit.

LISTENING AND SPEAKING SKILLS

> Annotating Lecture Notes
> Asking for Clarification
> **PRONUNCIATION** *Can* and *Can't*

Self-Assessment

Think about how well you know each target word, and check (✓) the appropriate column. I have…

TARGET WORDS	never seen this word before.	heard or seen the word but am not sure what it means.	heard or seen the word and understand what it means.	used the word confidently in *either* speaking or writing.
AWL				
🔑 conflict				
corporate				
edit				
🔑 equivalent				
🔑 guarantee				
🔑 obvious				
paragraph				
🔑 quote				
🔑 revise				
🔑 version				

🔑 Oxford 3000™ keywords

Vocabulary Activities

A. Cross out the word in each group that has a different meaning from the others.

1. ~~failure~~, guarantee, security, promise,
2. argument, agreement, conflict, fight
3. clear, obvious, plain, unusual,
4. form, song, version, type
5. different, equal, equivalent, similar
6. business, company, corporate, individual

B. Complete the paragraph with the target words from the box below.

guarantee	conflicts	obvious	equivalent	corporate

A company is sometimes called a(n) _____corporate_____ entity. In some ways,
(1)

laws treat companies as _____ to, or like, people even though there
(2)

are _____ differences between companies and people. For example,
(3)

people rarely live more than 100 years, but companies can last centuries. But,

like people, it's important for companies to have a good relationship with the

people they interact with, their customers, in order to stay in business. One

way they do that is by giving a _____ on products. They are, in effect,
(4)

promising that the product will be good. Another way companies keep their

customers happy is by avoiding _____. It's never a good idea to fight
(5)

with customers. There's a famous saying: "The customer is always right."

C. Work with a partner. Match the pairs that are equivalent.

_a_ 1. one kilometer   a. 0.62 miles
___ 2. 32 degrees Fahrenheit   b. 1,000 milliliters
___ 3. secondary school   c. 1,000 grams
___ 4. one liter   d. 0 degrees Celsius
___ 5. one kilogram   e. high school
___ 6. 6 feet   f. 1.83 meters

D. Work with a partner. Check (✓) the things that are obvious when you first meet someone. Then, with a partner, discuss other things that might be obvious when you first meet someone.

✓ hair color	☐ mother's name
☐ native language	☐ gender
☐ height	☐ age
☐ favorite book	☐ birthplace

To *conflict* (con-**FLICT**) means to disagree with or be different from someone or something.

> *John's version of events **conflicts** with yours.*

The verb can also mean to happen at the same time so you must choose one thing.

> *The lunch meeting **conflicts** with my English class.*

A *conflict* (**CON**-flict) is a fight or argument.

> *Mary often gets into **conflicts** with her boss.*

Or it can mean a difference between two or more ideas, wishes, etc.

> *The novel shows a **conflict** between love and duty.*

CORPUS

E. For each sentence, write *V* if the word *conflict* is a verb. Write *N* if *conflict* is a noun. Then read each sentence to a partner. Be sure to pronounce *conflict* as con-FLICT if it is used as a verb *or* CON-flict if it is used as a noun.

_V_ 1. That movie time conflicts with my dinner plans.

____ 2. Businesses that have conflicts over patents often go to court.

____ 3. Such conflicts can involve a lot of money.

____ 4. When a company's claim conflicts with the information on the patent application, the court may decide against them.

____ 5. The patent laws in some countries conflict occasionally with those in others.

____ 6. This can cause court outcomes to conflict depending on where the case comes to trial.

About the Topic

For centuries, people have considered new ideas to be similar to property. In other words, you can own an idea just as you can own a car or a farm. New ideas are important because they lead to discoveries (for example, the discovery of a drug for a new disease) and inventions (for example, the car or the television). Laws protect ideas from being stolen.

Before You Listen

Read these questions. Discuss your answers in a small group.

1. What are some products that you use every day? Do you know where the ideas for these products came from?

2. Who are some important inventors from history?

3. Why is it important to protect new ideas or products?

Listen

Read the Listen for Main Ideas activity below. Go online to listen to a lecture on patent law in different countries. A patent is a document that says the owner of the patent is the only person who can produce or use an invention.

Listen for Main Ideas

Read the questions about the audio. Work with a partner to ask and answer these questions.

1. What is the purpose of a patent?

2. How long have patents been around?

3. What do you need to get a patent?

4. Who does the patent go to in most countries?

5. Who does the patent go to in the United States?

NOTE-TAKING SKILL   Annotating Lecture Notes

LEARN

During a lecture or presentation in class, taking notes helps you remember key information. You can *annotate* your notes to better understand what you've written. When you annotate something, you add notes, headings, graphics, or other information to explain, clarify, and organize what is already written. Remember to leave extra space in your notes to add annotations later.

- Identify missing or unclear information.
- Add headings to organize information.
- Highlight main ideas and important details.

Look at the student's notes below. The second set of notes have been annotated by the student to help her organize the information.

Products: lights, TV, computer, phone

Inventor — new idea

Thomas Edison — first light bulb, 40,000 pages of notes, 1,600 materials

A patent protects the idea —

First patents date back hundreds of years

England 1300s

	PATENTS *Products: lights, TV, computer, phone* *Inventor — new idea* *Thomas Edison — first light bulb,* *40,000 pages of notes, 1,600 materials* *A patent protects the idea —* *guarantee for 20 years*
Purpose	*First patents date back hundreds of* *years*
History	*England 1300s*

APPLY

A. Listen to the lecture again. Work with a partner. Discuss the annotations that were made to the notes. How did the student make the notes easier to understand?

B. Go online and listen to the second half of the lecture. Add your notes to the student's notes above. Then listen to the lecture again. Annotate the notes you made. Compare your annotated notes with a partner's.

Vocabulary Activities

A. Complete the Word Form Chart below with the correct forms of the target words. Use a dictionary to check your answers. Some words may belong in more than one category.

| edit | editing | paragraph | quotation | quoted | revised |
| edited | editor | quotable | quote | revise | revision |

Word Form Chart		
Noun	**Verb**	**Adjective**
	edit	

B. Choose the best form of each target word to complete the sentences.

Armand: I need to make **edits** / **editors** on my paper before I turn it in.

Emma: Did you include any **quotations** / **quoted**?

Armand: I **quotation** / **quoted** two experts. What about you?

Emma: Yes, I've got some **quoted** / **quotation** stuff. When are the **revises** / **revisions** due?

Armand: Tomorrow. I'm going to **revision** / **revise** at the computer lab this afternoon.

Emma: If I come too, can you look my paper over? I could use a good **edits** / **editor**.

C. Complete the paragraph with the target vocabulary words from the box below.

| edit | quote | paragraph | revise |

The widespread use of the Internet makes it easier to copy the work of writers, musicians, and other artists. It has become a big problem. It is very easy to take someone else's writing if it appears on the Internet. People may do this without thinking they are doing something wrong. Sometimes

pressured students cut and paste a _paragraph_ or two from papers they
(1)
find online into their own essays. If someone else's writing is copied without

_____ it or making _____ to the text it is "plagiarism."
(2) (3)

Plagiarism is copying someone else's words and presenting them as your

own. It is illegal and is strictly enforced in many countries. Of course, it is

fine to _____ if you use the correct punctuation and give the name of
(4)

the person it belongs to.

D. Check (✓) the things that describe a paragraph. Explain your ideas to a partner.

☐ 20 sentences or more   ☐ is about one topic

☐ at least several sentences   ☐ every sentence is on a new line

☐ starts on a new line, but each   ☐ every sentence is numbered
sentence does not

☐ includes many ideas   ☐ uses a lot of abbreviations

E. The target word *edit* can have slightly different meanings depending on the context. Match the dictionary definitions on the left with the example sentences on the right.

edit (verb)

_b_ 1. to prepare a piece of writing by correcting mistakes and making it better

    a. She edits the online version of the *New York Times*.

___ 2. to prepare a book by collecting and arranging pieces by a number of different writers

    b. I need to edit my paper before I turn it in tomorrow.

___ 3. to make changes to text on a computer screen

    c. You can edit your work with the cut and paste keys.

___ 4. in a film or TV show, to decide which parts to include and in which order

    d. My tablet takes really good videos and I can edit them later.

___ 5. to plan and publish a newspaper, magazine, etc.

    e. Twenty poets are included in the book, but only one person edited it.

About the Topic

When does sharing something become stealing? It was legal in the 1990s to download music and share it with your friends. Then artists and recording companies found music that hadn't been officially released yet was already being shared for free on websites. Eventually it became illegal to do this.

Before You Watch

Read these questions. Discuss your answers in a small group.

1. What are some products that you have downloaded recently?

2. Is a song that you download considered property? Why or why not?

3. Why are there laws against downloading music or movies without paying?

Watch

Read the Listen for Main Ideas activity below.
Go online to watch three students as they review
and discuss their lecture notes on patents
and copyrights.

Listen for Main Ideas

Watch the video again. Work with a partner. Mark each sentence *P* if it describes
a patent, *C* if it describes a copyright, or *B* if it describes both.

_B_ 1. It protects the maker.

____ 2. It covers inventions, such as the light bulb.

____ 3. It covers art.

____ 4. It usually lasts for 20 years.

____ 5. It lasts for the lifetime of the maker plus 50 or 70 years.

SPEAKING SKILL Asking for Clarification

LEARN

In order to fully understand a lecture or presentation, you may need to ask the
speaker to clarify something he / she said. Often speakers will ask for questions
at the end of the lecture.

In a more informal group discussion, it is fine to politely interrupt and ask for
clarification during the discussion.

Some phrases for asking for clarification are:

Excuse me, could you explain ... ?

I'm sorry, what does ... mean?

I'm sorry, what is ... ?

What do you mean by ... ?

Is that the same as ... ?

Do you mean ... ?

APPLY

A. Go online to watch the video again. How does the speaker ask for clarification? Match each statement with the question that follows it.

_a_ 1. I hope everyone brought their notes on intellectual property.

___ 2. … inventions and designs, and the things you can get a copyright for, like artistic things.

___ 3. It's a guarantee that no one else can use their work.

___ 4. If you don't download music legally, you might actually have to pay a fine or even go to jail. It's stealing someone else's work.

    a. Intellectual property? What's that?

    b. I don't understand. Don't they want me to use it?

    c. Is that similar to plagiarism?

    d. I missed the part on copyright. Can you two explain it to me?

B. Work in groups of four. Each group member will choose one of the four concepts below. Review the unit and your notes to become the group "expert" on the concept. You may use your dictionaries. Prepare a one-minute explanation of the concept.

1. patent law in Europe
2. patent law in the United States
3. copyrights
4. plagiarism

C. Present your explanations. One group member presents at a time. The other three ask questions for clarification.

LEARN

A. You usually pronounce the word *can* with the reduced vowel /ə/. It is usually unstressed. Go online to listen to the sentences with the word *can*.

1. It is only worth the inventor's time if he or she *can* make some money from the idea.

2. *Can* we get some more help?

B. You usually pronounce the word *can't* with the vowel sound /æ/. It is lightly stressed. When a consonant sound follows, the /t/ can be faint. Pause briefly before making the next sound. Go online to listen to the sentences with the word *can't*.

1. They <u>can't</u> get one.

2. The idea <u>can't</u> appear obvious.

C. In each sentence, the word *can't* is stressed but is stressed less than the focus word in the sentence. Listen to the sentences.

1. You **can't** quote an entire **essay**.

2. So you **can't** use copyrighted **work**.

APPLY

A. Go online to listen to the sentences. Check if you hear *can* or *can't*.

1. can ☐ can't ☐   4. can ☐ can't ☐

2. can ☐ can't ☐   5. can ☐ can't ☐

3. can ☐ can't ☐   6. can ☐ can't ☐

B. Say the sentences from Learn, activities A, B, and C. Pronounce the appropriate vowel sound and use correct sentence stress.

C. With a partner, talk about what types of art form you are good at. For example, do you sing, play an instrument, paint, or make crafts? Use the words *can* and *can't* with the appropriate vowel sound and sentence stress.

> A: <u>Can</u> you play any **instruments**?
>
> B: I <u>can</u> play the **piano**, but I <u>can't</u> play it very **well**.

End of Unit Task

In this unit, you learned how to annotate notes to make them clearer and how to ask for clarification. Review these skills by taking notes on a new presentation. As you review, ask for clarification from your classmates.

A. Go online to listen to the presentation about intellectual property theft. Take notes, leaving room for annotations. Use the questions below as a guide.

- What is intellectual property theft?
- Who does it?
- Who is hurt by it?
- What is the speaker's opinion?

Intellectual Property Theft

B. Work with a group to review your notes and add annotations. Ask for and give clarification using these phrases:

Excuse me, could you explain ... ?

I'm sorry, what does ... mean?

I'm sorry, what is ... ?

What do you mean by ... ?

Is that the same as ... ?

Do you mean ... ?

C. Using your notes from activity A and from the other listening passages in this unit, discuss these questions with your group. Ask for and give clarification as needed.

1. How are patents and copyrights similar? How are they different?

2. Which should get more legal protection—an invention such as a cell phone, or an artistic work such as a painting or novel? Why?

3. Why do you think copyright protection lasts longer than a patent?

4. How does technology make it more difficult to protect artistic work? What are some ways to deal with this problem?

Self-Assessment		
Yes	**No**	
☐	☐	I successfully took notes and annotated them.
☐	☐	I asked for and gave clarification about the notes.
☐	☐	I participated in a group discussion using my annotated notes.
☐	☐	I can hear the difference between *can* and *can't* in natural speech.
☐	☐	I can correctly use the target vocabulary words from the unit.

Discussion Questions

With a partner or in a small group, discuss the following questions.

1. Why do laws protect people who invent things?

2. Do you think patents in one country should apply to all countries?

3. How long do you think a patent should last?

UNIT 8

What Your Brain Says about You

In this unit, you will

> learn about what MRIs can tell us about the brain.

> increase your understanding of the target academic words for this unit.

LISTENING AND SPEAKING SKILLS

> Recognizing Language That Signals a Definition
> Organizing a Short Presentation
> **PRONUNCIATION** Stress in Phrasal Verbs

Self-Assessment

Think about how well you know each target word, and check (✓) the appropriate column. I have…

TARGET WORDS	never seen this word before.	heard or seen the word but am not sure what it means.	seen or heard the word and understand what it means.	used the word confidently in *either* speaking or writing.
AWL				
compute				
🔑 confirm				
🔑 constant				
🔑 deny				
🔑 encounter				
evaluate				
🔑 fundamental				
🔑 odd				
specify				
🔑 volume				

🔑 Oxford 3000™ keywords

Vocabulary Activities

A. Complete the Word Form Chart below with the correct forms of the target words. Use a dictionary to check your answers.

computable	compute	computer	computation
computerized	confirm	confirmed	confirmation
deniable	denial	deny	fundamentally
specified	specify	specifiable	undeniably

Word Form Chart			
Nouns	**Verbs**	**Adjectives**	**Adverbs**
		computable	
			_____
			_____
_____			_____

B. Complete the paragraph below with the correct forms of the target words from activity A. Use the words in parentheses to help you.

The _____*fundamental*_____ purpose of an MRI is to look at the brain.
(1 . important or basic)

An MRI can _____ if a patient has cancer. It can even
(2. say is true)

_____ where and how big the cancer is. The scan is
(3. in detail)

_____ evidence of the problem. Much of the technology
(4. cannot be shown to be false)

doctors use today is _____ so they are less likely to make
(5. operated by computer)

mistakes. Without such technology, medical professionals might have to treat

a(n) _____ problem. Now, technology such as an MRI
(6. not clearly stated)

is a _____ of the doctor's best guess. It can save time
(7. statement that something is true)

and money.

C. For each of the following items, match the topic with what you need to specify.

Topic

_c_ 1. your next doctor's appointment

____ 2. the location of a store

____ 3. a sweater

____ 4. oranges on your grocery list

____ 5. a research paper

____ 6. a book at the library

What you need to specify

a. the topic and number of pages

b. the address

c. the date and time

d. how many

e. the size and color

f. the title and author

D. To *deny* is to say something is false, to refuse to accept something, or to refuse permission. To *confirm* is to say that something is true. Work with a partner. Read each quote below. Is the person confirming or denying? Write *C* (confirm) or *D* (deny).

_C_ 1. "Yes, that's right. Your appointment is at 3 p.m."

____ 2. "No, that's not quite true. I didn't miss the entire lecture."

____ 3. "You're correct. Just by looking at the images of the brain, we can tell what the person is remembering."

____ 4. "I'm sorry to tell you this, but you can't leave early today."

____ 5. "I don't know anything about that."

____ 6. "It's exactly what you thought."

E. *Fundamental* means "important or basic." Which of the following is fundamental to you in an English class? Check the boxes. Then tell a partner.

☐ the time

☐ the classroom

☐ the instructor's teaching style

☐ the textbook

☐ the topics

☐ the other students

☐ the amount of discussion

☐ the teacher's education

About the Topic

Neuroscience is the study of how the brain works. Until recently, scientists and doctors could only study a human brain after somebody died. New technology such as CAT scans and MRIs have changed this. During many brain operations, the surgeon is talking with the patient during the surgery to make sure that the brain is not being harmed. The patient is awake but in no pain.

Before You Listen

Read these questions. Discuss your answers in a small group.

1. Have you ever seen a brain scan?

2. What do you want to know about your brain?

3. Do you think companies should develop technology that can help them see what people are thinking?

Listen

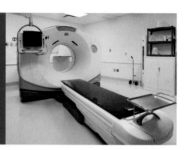

Read the Listen for Main Ideas activity below. Go online to listen to a radio report about new technology and the amazing insights it is giving neuroscientists about the human brain.

Listen for Main Ideas

Mark each sentence as *T* (true) or *F* (false). Work with a partner. Restate false sentences to make them correct.

__T__ 1. Neuroscientists study the brain.

____ 2. A functional MRI shows which parts of the brain are active.

____ 3. MRIs measure the amount of blood in the brain.

____ 4. A computer can tell what someone is looking at because of the activity in the brain.

____ 5. Researchers can tell what someone is going to think next.

LISTENING SKILL   Recognizing Language That Signals a Definition

LEARN

When you listen to lectures, radio reports, presentations, and television programs, you will hear new words. You might not have time to look them up in a dictionary. However, the speaker will often explain the definitions.

Some words will signal that the speaker is going to define a term. Learning these signal words will help you understand a talk about a topic that is new to you. See the chart on page 89 for examples of some words that signal a definition.

Signal words	Example sentences
is / are	A scan is a picture of something.
which is	Neuroscience, which is the study of how the brain works, is a growing field.
refers to	Magnetic resonance imaging refers to the scans that scientists make of the activity in the brain.
is / are defined as	MRIs use contrast agents. These are defined as substances that show the structures in the body.
that is	A scan, that is, the picture the machine takes of your brain, …

APPLY

A. Go online to listen to the radio report again. Circle the signal words you hear.

refers to	which is	that is
is defined as	stands for	is / are

B. Listen to the radio report again. Match each word or phrase to its definition.

_d_ 1. MRI

_____ 2. a functional MRI

_____ 3. neurons

_____ 4. a rich episodic memory

a. something that happened to you or where you can remember the place, the people, the time, and other details

b. images that show brain activity by measuring changes in the oxygen level of the blood in the brain

c. the nerve cells that carry information in our brains

d. magnetic resonance imaging

C. Work with a partner. Retell as much of the report as you can using the words and phrases in activity B above. Use signal words as you speak.

Vocabulary Activities

A. Look at the groups of words in each column. For each group, write the target word that has a similar meaning.

constant	encounter	evaluate	odd	volume

volume	_____	_____	_____	_____
size	meet	judge	unusual	always
amount	experience	think about	different	never-ending
loudness	find		strange	repeatedly

B. Work with a partner. Complete the sentences using the correct form of the target words you added to the chart in activity A.

Albert Einstein was a genius—someone much more intelligent than

the average person. Shortly after his death, his brain was removed and

photographed. Recently, researchers ___evaluated___ the photos to learn more
                                          (1)

about Einstein's brain. The pictures show his brain was the same general size,

or _____ , as most brains, perhaps a little smaller. However, it was a
        (2)

little _____ in other ways. The researchers had never _____
          (3)   (4)

a brain with as many folds as Einstein's. The unusual features of his brain

may explain his genius and our _____ fascination with Einstein and
                                      (5)

his ideas.

When you *evaluate* something, you form an opinion of the amount, value, or
quality of something after thinking about it carefully.

> We **evaluated** the situation carefully before we made our decision.

It is often followed by the nouns *effectiveness, effect, accuracy, usefulness,
significance, performance,* and *outcome.*

CORPUS

C. Select the phrase in the second column that best completes each sentence.

_b_ 1. The Food and Drug Administration evaluates

a. job performance.

___ 2. Once a year, the supervisor evaluates

b. the effectiveness of medication.

___ 3. MRIs can help doctors evaluate

c. the accuracy of a diagnosis of cancer.

D. Some words have more than one definition. For the target words below, match the dictionary definitions on the left with the example sentences on the right.

odd (adjective)

Definitions

_d_ 1. strange or unusual

___ 2. not frequent

___ 3. various, different sizes and shapes

___ 4. not matching

Example Sentences

a. He built a toaster out of odd parts he found around the house.

b. I'll use the odd plate since we only have eight of the set.

c. He makes the odd mistake, but he usually does pretty well.

d. He has the oddest habit—he sings all of his answers in class.

volume (noun)

Definitions

___ 1. a book

___ 2. the amount

___ 3. the amount of sound

Example Sentences

a. Can you turn the volume down? I can't hear anything else.

b. They've added more roads to handle the growing volume of traffic.

c. The library has more than 200,000 volumes.

E. Which of the things below do you wish could be constantly available to you? Why? Discuss your ideas with a partner.

your cell phone	food	Wi-Fi	electricity
your best friend	water	email	music

About the Topic

Memory may seem simple, but it is a complex and important process in the brain. Memory is part of recognizing what we see, hear, and read. Once we learn what an object is, we don't have to learn it again. Our brain remembers what it looks like or sounds like—often in more than one language.

Before You Watch

Read these questions. Discuss your answers in a small group.

1. What do you do when you have to memorize information?

2. What different study strategies have you used?

3. Have you ever taught someone else a study or memorization strategy?

Watch

Read the Listen for Main Ideas activity below. Go online to watch a presentation on how the brain memorizes information.

Listen for Main Ideas

Read the questions about the video. Work with a partner to ask and answer these questions.

1. How can the shapes of letters help some people memorize facts?

2. What information is contained in the name *Roy G. Biv*?

3. What different types of memories can the brain hold?

4. What are the two things that could happen to short-term memories stored in the hippocampus?

PRESENTATION SKILL   Organizing a Short Presentation

LEARN

When you're giving a short presentation, here are some suggested guidelines:

1. Focus on no more than three main ideas.

2. Present the main ideas in the introduction, and then summarize them in the conclusion.

3. Use sequence words and phrases to signal your main ideas.

4. Give details or examples that support each main idea.

There are different ways to organize your main ideas:

• Least important to most important

• Most important to least important (news stories)

• Time order (first to last)

• Space (things closer to things farther away)

APPLY

A. Watch the presentation again. Complete the outline by putting the statements below in the correct order.

a. take a nap

b. uses part of the brain that identifies what the eye sees

c. sleeping moves memories from hippocampus to neocortex

d. verbal elaboration: make up a word or sentence

e. lets you memorize a smaller amount of information

f. neocortex stores long-term memories

g. uses part of the brain involved with language

h. hippocampus stores short-term memories

i. ~~visual inspection: memorize shape or color~~

j. some people remember shapes better than words

_i_ Main point 1

___ Supporting detail

___ Supporting detail

___ Main point 2

___ Supporting detail

___ Supporting detail

___ Main point 3

___ Supporting detail

___ Supporting detail

B. Choose one of the topics below, or a topic of your choice. Make an outline of a presentation with three main ideas. Decide how you will organize the three ideas and add details. Then share your ideas with a partner. Revise your outline after you get feedback.

How technology has changed our everyday lives.

How to be a good student.

How to raise happy, productive children.

How to be a good teacher.

C. Work in small groups. Take turns giving a short presentation on your topic for three minutes as the other group members take notes. Then ask your group members to name your three main ideas and how they are organized.

Main Point 1: _____

Details: _____

Main Point 2: _____

Details: _____

Main Point 3: _____

Details: _____

How is the presentation organized?

_____

PRONUNCIATION SKILL | Stress in Phrasal Verbs

LEARN

A. A phrasal verb is a phrase that includes a verb and a word that looks like a preposition. A phrasal verb has a different meaning than the verb by itself. Go online to listen to some examples of common phrasal verbs and their meanings.

Phrasal verb	Meaning
ask around	ask several people the same question
bring up	start talking about something
check out	investigate something new
figure out	realize or come to a conclusion
grow up	get older
let down	not help or support someone
look over	examine, review, or inspect
think back	remember something

B. In a phrasal verb, you stress the second word. You often link sounds when using phrasal verbs. When a verb ends in a consonant sound and the following preposition or adverb begins with a vowel, link the two sounds together. Go online to listen. Notice the stressed word in pink.

We'll have to see if this technology brings about a fundamental change in the way people relate to one another.

APPLY

A. Go online to listen to the examples of phrasal verbs. Insert linking marks below the sounds that should be linked.

1. ask around
2. bring up
3. check out
4. figure out
5. grow up
6. look over

B. Say the phrasal verbs from Apply, activity A. Stress the second word and link the appropriate sounds.

C. Work with a partner. Write sentences using the meanings of the phrasal verbs from the chart in Learn, activity A. Then your partner will guess which phrasal verb you are talking about. In the response, link the sounds and stress the preposition. Then switch roles.

> A: I'm going to review my essay and make sure that there are no
>   punctuation errors.
>
> B: Look **over**.

End of Unit Task

In this unit, you learned how to listen for definitions in speaking. You also learned how to organize a presentation around three main points. Review these skills by giving and listening to short presentations.

A. You will give a two-minute presentation to a group. Choose one of the topics below or use your own ideas. Select a topic you haven't presented on before.

How technology has changed our lives.

How to be a good student.

How to raise happy, productive children.

How to be a good teacher.

B. Prepare a short introduction. Answer these questions.

- What three main ideas will you cover?
- Why is this topic interesting or important?

C. Write the three main ideas on the outline below (which continues on page 96). Add notes and details below each main idea. List any vocabulary or terms you think might be new.

Main Idea 1: _____

_____

Details: _____

_____

New Vocabulary: _____

Main Idea 2: _____

_____

Details: _____

_____

New Vocabulary: _____

Main Idea 3: _____

_____

Details: _____

_____

New Vocabulary: _____

D. Prepare a conclusion. Remember to summarize your three main points. Remember to explain new vocabulary using the signal words and phrases in the box below.

is / are	which is	refers to	is defined as	that is

E. With your group, take turns giving your presentations. As you listen to your group member's presentations, take notes. Write down any definitions you hear. Then ask for clarification to make sure you understand the main points.

Self-Assessment		
Yes	**No**	
☐	☐	I recognized language that signaled a definition.
☐	☐	I defined new vocabulary as necessary.
☐	☐	I can use stress in phrasal verbs correctly.
☐	☐	I organized a two-minute presentation using three main points.
☐	☐	I can correctly use the target vocabulary words from the unit.

Discussion Questions

With a partner or in a small group, discuss the following questions.

1. What is an MRI?

2. Do you consider Dr. Campos's computer to be "reading a mind"?

3. Do you think it's easier to memorize information when studying alone or as part of a study group? Why?

UNIT 9

Protecting Our Oceans

In this unit, you will

> learn about efforts to save declining coral reefs.
> learn about eco-tourism in endangered areas.
> increase your understanding of the target academic words in this unit.

LISTENING AND SPEAKING SKILLS

> Listening for Specific Information
> Giving Advice and Making Recommendations
> **PRONUNCIATION** Asking with Tag Questions

Self-Assessment

Think about how well you know each target word, and check (✓) the appropriate column. I have…

TARGET WORDS	never seen this word before.	heard or seen the word but am not sure what it means.	heard or seen the word and understand what it means.	used the word confidently in *either* speaking or writing.
AWL				
🔑 annual				
🔑 consist				
🔑 contribute				
🔑 decade				
🔑 decline				
🔑 distribute				
🔑 foundation				
maximize				
minimal				
🔑 project				

 Oxford 3000™ keywords

Vocabulary Activities

Word Form Chart		
Noun	**Verb**	**Adjective**
decade	_____	_____
decline	decline	declining
foundation		
project projection	project	projected

A. Complete the sentences using the correct form of the target words in the Word Form Chart.

Over the last few _____*decades*_____, our climate has been changing. In effect, the
                    (1)

world is becoming warmer. Some plants and animals will continue to do well,

but others will not. For example, the number of polar bears is _____
                                                                (2)

as the ice is decreasing. When the ice melts, the bears have to swim longer

and longer distances to find food. Many organizations are trying to help the

polar bear. The World Wildlife Fund is one _____ that tries to save
                                           (3)

animals that are in danger. They have many _____ that people can
                                           (4)

support with donations. These groups often try to restore, or bring back, the

conditions that the animals need to survive.

B. Cross out the word that has a different meaning from the others. Use your
dictionary to help you. Check your answers with a partner.

1. decrease, decline, drop, ~~grow~~
2. project, group, colleagues, coworkers
3. foundation, scientist, institute, corporation
4. growth, projection, foundation, extension
5. decline, agree, confirm, accept
6. years, decade, ocean, period

C. Some words have multiple meanings. For the target words below, match the dictionary definitions on the left with the example sentences on the right.

foundation (noun)

Definitions

_b_ 1. the bricks and concrete that form the base of a building

___ 2. a principle, idea, or fact that something is based on

___ 3. an organization that provides money for a certain purpose

___ 4. the act of starting a new institution or organization

___ 5. a skin-colored cream that is used on the face, usually under other makeup

Example Sentences

a. Respect is the foundation of a strong marriage.

b. The explosion shook the foundation of the buildings nearby.

c. I don't like to use foundation or any other makeup; it isn't good for my skin.

d. The club has grown a lot since its foundation 20 years ago.

e. That foundation supports research on cancer.

Project can be both a noun and a verb, with multiple meanings. When it is a noun, the stress is on the first syllable (**pro**-ject).

*We're working on group **projects** in class today.*

When it is a verb, the stress is on the second syllable (pro-**ject**).

*You really need to **project** your voice in that lecture hall or the students won't hear you.*

CORPUS

project (noun, verb)

Definitions

_c_ 1. a planned piece of work designed to find information

___ 2. a piece of work involving careful study by students

___ 3. to estimate size, cost, or amounts of something in the future based on the present

___ 4. to make light or an image fall on a flat surface, like a screen

___ 5. to stick out from an edge or surface

Example Sentences

a. They projected a decrease in gas prices but prices went up instead.

b. The organization is doing a research project on coral.

c. What topic did you choose for your biology project?

d. Can we project the presentation onto the board?

e. The top floor of the building projects out over the street.

D. A *decade* is a period of ten years. With a partner, name one thing that was popular or that happened during each of the decades below.

| 1950s | 1960s | 1970s | 1980s | 1990s | 2000–2010 |

"Someone walked on the moon for the first time in the 1960s."

About the Topic

With climate change, the oceans are getting warmer. The changing temperature affects many of the plants and animals that live in the ocean. Some kinds of plants and animals grow too rapidly in the warmer water, while others begin to die.

Before You Watch

Read these questions. Discuss your answers in a small group.

1. Have you ever gone diving in the ocean?

2. Have you seen a coral reef?

3. What do you most enjoy about the ocean?

⊘ Watch

Read the Listen for Main Ideas activity below. Go online to watch a news report about **declining** coral reefs and how people are trying to help regrow the coral.

⊘ Listen for Main Ideas

Read the questions about the video. Work with a partner to ask and answer these questions.

_b_ 1. What is causing the problems with coral reefs?

    a. tiny animals

    b. climate change

    c. research teams

___ 2. What will happen if the coral reefs die?

    a. It will hurt tourism.

    b. There will be too many fish.

    c. The ocean will warm up.

___ 3. How do scientists grow new coral?

    a. They make it in a lab.

    b. They use drugs.

    c. They cut off pieces of other coral.

___ 4. What is one benefit of coral?

    a. It is a good source of food.

    b. It keeps sharks away.

    c. It protects beaches.

___ 5. What is one thing Niedermeyer needs now?

    a. money

    b. new laws

    c. permission to continue

LEARNING SKILL | Listening for Specific Information

LEARN

In a lecture, presentation, or broadcast, the main ideas are usually followed by specific information. This can be details such as names, numbers, dates, and places or reasons, explanations, or examples. Here are some signal words that signal specific information.

Specific information	Signal words
Numbers	*percent, year*
Names of people or groups	*named, called*
Examples	*for example, for instance, like, such as*
Reasons	*because, cause, due to, because of*
Places	*coast of, city of, state of, near, in, on*

APPLY

A. Go online to watch the video again. Complete the sentences with the information you hear. Check your answers with a partner.

1. Climate change could damage _____ % of the world's coral by the year _____ .

2. Coral are tiny organisms living on limestone that Niedermeyer is growing off the coast of _____ .

3. Because of disease, _____, and warming ocean temperatures, coral coverage has decreased from about _____ % 30 years ago to _____ % today.

4. Every _____ months, they cut the ends off healthy coral and plant them in the ocean.

5. Niedermeyer recently received permission from the _____ to plant _____ pieces of coral on protected reefs.

6. His group is called the _____ .

7. He only has enough _____ to keep operations running through _____ .

Vocabulary Activities

A. Work with a partner. After each word or phrase, write the word from the box below that has an opposite meaning. Use your dictionary to check your answers.

annual	consist	contribute	distribute	minimal	maximize

1. be empty of _____consist_____

2. collect, keep _____

3. take away _____

4. most _____

5. daily _____

6. make smaller _____

B. Complete the paragraph below with the correct form of the target words from activity A.

Some students' usual break from school _____consists_____ of watching TV
                                            (1)

and playing video games. But with a _____ amount of work, they
                                         (2)

could have an amazing vacation. They can _____ their fun by trying
                                               (3)

something new and adventurous. They can take a volunteer vacation. Many

organizations allow people to volunteer on interesting projects. These projects

usually _____ something to a local community. For example, you can
            (4)

volunteer with Habitat for Humanity and build a house in another country.

Some organizations _____ food or medical supplies. When you are
                         (5)

planning your _____ summer vacation, check out volunteer vacations.
                   (6)

C. Some words are formal and others are more informal. Complete the chart with the formal target words, and the informal word or phrase with a similar meaning. Then use your dictionary to check your work.

Formal	Informal
1.	yearly
2. consist	
3. contribute	
4.	hand out
5.	increase
6. minimal	

The verb *contribute* has several meanings:

1. Together with others, to give a part of the total.

   *Would you like to **contribute** toward the present for Lydia?*

2. To be one of the causes of something.

   *Poor communication **contributed** to the problem in the company.*

3. To write articles for a magazine or newspaper.

   *He has **contributed** articles to several magazines.*

CORPUS

D. For each of the sentences below, write the number [1–3] for the meaning of *contribute* that the sentence uses.

_1_ 1. I plan to contribute to an organization that helps save coral reefs.

____ 2. Everyone on the project contributed to its success.

____ 3. Global warming contributes to the decline of coral reefs.

____ 4. She contributes essays regularly to publications about the environment.

____ 5. Coral reefs contribute to tourism by providing protection to beaches.

____ 6. If five more people contribute, we can get a new coffeemaker for the office.

About the Topic

Vacation is often simply a time to relax. However, people also use their vacations as a chance to learn about a different culture or to be in a new natural environment. Tour companies are creating environmentally friendly tours and volunteer opportunities to give travelers unique vacation experiences.

Before You Listen

Read these questions. Discuss your answers in a small group.

1. Where do you like to travel? Why?
2. What do tourists do when they visit your country?
3. Do you think tourism helps your city or country? Why or why not?

Listen

Read the Listen for Main Ideas activity below. Go online to listen to the radio broadcast of a talk on the benefits of ecotourism for tourists and the countries they visit.

Listen for Main Ideas

Read the questions about ecotourism. Work with a partner to ask and answer these questions.

__c__ 1. Ecotourism is travel that helps ___.

    a. cities   b. restaurants   c. the environment

____ 2. Visitors should use ___.

    a. little energy   b. bus tours   c. sports equipment

____ 3. Ecotourism is ___ annually.

    a. declining   b. growing   c. staying the same

____ 4. Countries like ___ have a lot of ecotourism.

    a. the U.S. and the UK   b. Costa Rica and Belize   c. Bolivia and Japan

____ 5. ___ lets you stay with local people in their homes.

    a. Community-based   b. Volunteer vacations   c. A cruise ship
        tourism

SPEAKING SKILL   Giving Advice and Making Recommendations

LEARN

There are several ways to give advice and make recommendations. You can use modals and other expressions for suggestions. You can also use *I suggest* or *I recommend* before advice. Imperatives can be used for advice and recommendations, but they sound much stronger.

Modals	I suggest / recommend ...	Imperatives
You should go to Belize.	I suggest (that) you look into Belize.	Go see the animals.
You might try ecotours.		Try staying with local people.
You could get information online.	I recommend (that) you try ecotours.	
	Why don't you visit a travel agency?	

You can support your advice or suggestions with facts, research results, or your own experience. This makes your recommendations more powerful.

APPLY

A. Go online to listen to the talk again. Write the expressions you hear. Write an "X" on the line if you hear an imperative. Correct capitalization if necessary.

1. _____ *I suggest you* _____ check out an ecotourism trip that gives you a chance to volunteer in the local community. ____

2. _____ also look at community-based tourism. ____

3. _____ go on an ecotour! ____

B. Go online to listen again. Write the information the speaker gives to support each recommendation in activity A.

1. _____

2. _____

3. _____

C. Work with a partner. For each suggestion below, give supporting information to convince someone to follow the suggestion.

1. You should give money to help the coral reefs.

    "Coral reef coverage has decreased from 50% to 7% in the last 30 years."

2. You should visit a coral reef sometime soon.

3. I recommend taking an ecotourism vacation.

D. Choose one of the topics below. Take notes on information you can use to support your advice and recommendations. Then present your advice and recommendations to a small group. Speak for at least two minutes.

Decline in the number of rainforests

Good ways to help the environment in your daily life

Best places to visit on a vacation

LEARN

A. Tag questions are short questions that follow a statement. The statement before a tag question receives falling intonation. Then you pause (|) between the statement and tag. If the speaker is making small talk and looking for the listener to agree, the tag question also receives falling intonation. Go online to listen.

1. He has planned an ecotourism trip, | hasn't he? I knew it was something he wanted to do.

2. Pollution is a real problem for the community, | isn't it? New laws need to be made.

B. If the speaker is asking for confirmation and is uncertain of the answer, the tag question receives rising intonation. Go online to listen.

1. He wasn't going to leave the foundation, | was he? They still need his help there.

2. The decline hasn't gotten worse over the last decade, | has it? The team has been working so hard to save the reefs.

APPLY

A. Go online to listen to the sentences. Using the intonation that you hear, check (✓) the speaker's purpose. Check your answers.

	Asking for agreement / Making small talk	Asking for confirmation
1. You'll meet lots of new people on your trip, won't you?	✓	
2. The project will be hard work, won't it?		
3. The annual cost is very high, isn't it?		
4. Finding volunteers has been a challenge, hasn't it?		
5. He didn't vote against the new pollution laws, did he?		
6. They're really looking forward to the trip, aren't they?		

B. Work with a partner. Say the examples from Learn, activities A and B. Be sure to use correct intonation.

C. With a partner, discuss if you would want to go on an ecotourism trip. Talk about where you would go. Ask for your partner's opinions by using tag questions. Be sure to use appropriate intonation.

> A: *Volunteering on a farm sounds interesting, doesn't it? I've always wanted to know what it would be like.*
>
> B: *I don't know. Working on a farm is a lot of hard work, isn't it?*
>
> A: *It probably would be, but you would learn a lot, wouldn't you?*

End of Unit Task

In this unit, you learned how to recognize language that signals specific information and how to give advice and ask for recommendations. Review these skills by listening for specific information in a new audio, and talking with tourists about a new place. As you review, give advice and ask for recommendations from your classmates.

A. Look at the photo. Would you like to visit Palau? Why or why not? Tell a partner.

B. Read the comprehension questions. Then go online to listen to the podcast about ecotourism in Palau. Work with a partner to discuss the questions.

1. Where is Palau?

   _____

2. Why is tourism important in Palau?

   _____

3. What is one environmental law there?

   _____

4. How much did tourism increase in 2011?

_____

5. What is the price of swimming with the jellyfish?

_____

C. With a partner or in small group, role-play giving advice and recommendations to travelers who are going to Palau. Switch roles and repeat. Use expressions like the ones in the chart.

Modals	I suggest / recommend:	Imperatives
You should …	I suggest (that) you …	Go swimming with the jellyfish.
You might …	I recommend (that) you …	
You could …	I recommend …	Try staying with local people.
	Why don't you …	

D. With a partner, discuss recommendations you could make to the government of Palau. Give reasons to support your recommendations.

"Build a small aquarium so tourists can interact with the jellyfish, but won't pollute the water."

Self-Assessment		
Yes	**No**	
☐	☐	I successfully listened for specific information.
☐	☐	I practiced giving advice and recommendations.
☐	☐	I practiced the target vocabulary in the unit.
☐	☐	I can use correct intonation in tag questions.
☐	☐	I can correctly use the target vocabulary words from the unit.

Discussion Questions

With a partner or in a small group, discuss the following questions.

1. What can we do to save the coral reefs?

2. Would you consider taking an eco-friendly tour instead of a regular vacation?

3. Do you believe some places should be off-limits to people?

Inventing Our Future

In this unit, you will

> learn about advances in robotic technology.
> learn about artificial organs.
> increase your understanding of the target academic words for this unit.

LISTENING AND SPEAKING SKILLS

> Listening for Reasons and Explanations
> Paraphrasing Experts to Support Opinions
> **PRONUNCIATION** Using Stress in Chunking and Sentence Focus

Self-Assessment

Think about how well you know each target word, and check (✓) the appropriate column. I have…

TARGET WORDS	never seen this word before.	heard or seen the word but am not sure what it means.	heard or seen the word and understand what it means.	used the word confidently in *either* speaking or writing.
AWL				
exceed				
flexible				
🔑 internal				
journal				
🔑 maintain				
🔑 medium				
🔑 minimum				
🔑 option				
🔑 reject				
submit				

🔑 Oxford 3000™ keywords

Vocabulary Activities

A. The following target words have multiple meanings. Read the sentences. Write the number of the correct definition for the word in bold.

exceed *(verb)* **1** to be greater than a particular number or amount; **2** to do more than what is allowed or necessary

flexible *(adj)* **1** able to change to suit new conditions or situations; **2** able to move or bend easily without breaking

internal *(adj)* **1** of or on the inside of a place, person or object; **2** happening or existing inside an organization, country, etc.

option *(noun)* **1** the freedom to choose; **2** a thing that you choose or can choose; **3** something you can choose to have in a new car, truck, etc., but must pay for

_2_ 1. He was **exceeding** the speed limit.

___ 2. The price of the ticket shouldn't **exceed** $50.

___ 3. Are your work hours **flexible**?

___ 4. She is really **flexible** because she does a lot of yoga.

___ 5. Doctors use X-rays to see **internal** organs.

___ 6. **Internal** emails showed that workers were using the Internet for personal use.

___ 7. I don't have any **option**—my parents have told me I have to work.

___ 8. **Options** for the car include heated seats, a GPS, and a music system.

B. For each item below, write *F* if you think it should be *flexible* and *I* if you think it should be *inflexible*. Then explain your reasons to a partner.

___ driving laws ___ building materials ___ class schedules

___ exercise instructors ___ supervisors ___ cell phone covers

___ parents ___ skis ___ guard rails on highways

C. Check (✓) the things on your body that are internal.

✓ stomach	☐ lungs
☐ hair	☐ heart
☐ brain	☐ skin
☐ fingernails	☐ eyebrows

D. Match the category with its options. Compare answers with a partner.

_a_ 1. college course   a. English 101, Math 320, Biology 122

English 101, Math 320, and Biology 122 are college course options.

___ 2. vacation spot   b. yoga, walking, swimming

___ 3. exercise   c. print, save, open, close

___ 4. news source   d. the Caribbean, Europe, Bali

___ 5. computer menu bar   e. TV, magazines, the Internet, newspapers

About the Topic

Scientists developed exoskeletons to help people with severe injuries to move again. The person wears the exoskeleton on his / her arms and legs, and also wears a special hat. When the person thinks about moving, there is electrical activity in the brain. The hat senses the electrical activity, and gives commands to the exoskeleton on how to move.

Before You Watch

Read these questions. Discuss your answers in a small group.

1. Have you ever seen a robot? If so, what did it do?
2. What are the most useful things robots can do for people?
3. What things do you own now that follow your commands?

Watch

Read the Listen for Main Ideas activity below. Go online to watch a news report about a young man who was paralyzed after a car accident and how robotic technology helped him.

Listen for Main Ideas

Read the questions about the video. Work with a partner to ask and answer these questions.

1. What is Austin's problem?
2. Who helped Austin?
3. What did they build?
4. What did it help him do?
5. What event were they getting ready for?

LISTENING SKILL   Listening for Reasons and Explanations

LEARN

To hear and understand a speaker's reasons and explanations, listen for certain words or phrases that signal reasons or causes.

	Result (or effect)	Reason (or cause)
because	I can't come to class	because I'm sick today.
because of	Coral reefs are dying	because of global warming.
since	It's OK to use the quote	since you use quotation marks.
The / One reason is	One reason I can't study tonight is	I have to work.

APPLY

A. In each of the following sentences, underline the cause. If there is a signal word or phrase, circle it.

1. The game was rescheduled (because of) the rain.
2. It was raining really hard. We rescheduled the game for Saturday.
3. The reason I'm late is that I missed the bus.
4. I studied all weekend. I got an excellent final grade.
5. Since she's injured, she has to use crutches.

B. Go online to watch the video again and complete the sentences. Include any words or phrases that signal reasons or causes. Then write two more sentences.

1. Austin is paralyzed *because of a car accident* _____ .

   _____ .

2. People are able to walk _____

   _____

   _____ .

3. The reason it was a good idea to have Austin working in the lab was _____

   _____

   _____ .

4. They wanted to finish the exoskeleton quickly _____

   _____

   _____ .

5. Other paralyzed people have reason to hope because _____

   _____

   _____ .

C. Work with a partner. Retell the story in the video. Include the following information.

1. The reason Austin is paralyzed.
2. The reason the professor is working on robotic exoskeletons.
3. The purpose of a skeleton (internal / external).
4. The reason they worked quickly on this project.
5. The effects of his walking across the stage.

Vocabulary Activities

Word Form Chart		
Noun	**Verb**	**Adjective**
journal	journal	_____
maintenance	maintain	maintained
minimum	_____	_____
rejection	reject	rejected
submission	submit	submitted

A. Complete the paragraph with the correct form of the target words in the Word Form Chart. Use a dictionary to help you understand new words.

My uncle recently received a heart transplant. He had heart disease for many years and was very weak. His doctors ___submitted___ his case to the transplant
(1)
center for consideration. They have guidelines they have to follow. They

nearly _____ him because of his age, but he just made the age limit
(2)
at 70. The transplant center said he needed to have a _____ of two
(3)
caretakers after he left the hospital. Transplant patients need a lot of help. A

caretaker helps the patient _____ a routine after surgery, including
(4)
taking medicine and following a healthy diet. He also needed to keep a

_____ about his feelings. There are emotional challenges when you
(5)
get a heart transplant. Writing in a journal helps relieve some of the stress.

B. Check (✓) the things you would reject, or not accept. Then share your ideas with a partner.

____ 1. a job with no health insurance

____ 2. a college without sports teams

____ 3. an opinion that didn't agree with mine

____ 4. an invitation to go to a rock concert

____ 5. an expensive gift from a person I have only known a short time

C. The word *medium* has multiple meanings. Match the dictionary definitions on the left with the example sentences on the right.

medium (adjective, noun)

Definitions

_c_ 1. in the middle, between two sizes, amounts, etc.

____ 2. a way of communicating information to people

____ 3. something that is used for a particular purpose

____ 4. the material or form that an artist, writer, or musician uses

____ 5. a substance that something exists or grows in

Example Sentences

a. They grew the new windpipe in a medium of preexisting cells.

b. The medium of television has only existed since the 20th century.

c. I am of medium height, but my sister is tall.

d. That artist likes to work with oils—it's his favorite medium.

e. English is the medium of instruction.

D. Work with a partner. Put a check (✓) below each verb in the chart headings that can "be done" to the noun in the last column.

Maintain	Reject	Submit	
			a lawn
			an application
			a road
			one's innocence
			an idea
			a transplanted organ
			plans
			report
			suggestion

About the Topic

The first artificial body part is at least 3000 years old. Scientists found an artificial toe attached to a skeleton in an Egyptian tomb. The artificial toe was made from leather and wood. People have used wooden, metal, and plastic replacements for feet, legs, hands, and arms. Within the last century, researchers have developed other artificial parts, including organs such as the heart, lungs, and kidneys.

Before You Listen

Read these questions. Discuss your answers in a small group.

1. Do you know anyone with an artificial organ?

2. If you lost your hand, would you want an artificial one? Why or why not?

3. Do you think scientists will ever create artificial body parts that work as well as original body parts?

Listen

Read the Listen for Main Ideas activity below. Go online to listen to three students discuss artificial organs.

Listen for Main Ideas

Listen to the audio and check (✓) the topics the speakers discuss. Then compare your answers with a partner.

- ☐ the definition of an artificial organ
- ☐ benefits of organs grown on scaffolds
- ☐ statistics on the numbers of artificial organs
- ☐ disadvantages of artificial hands
- ☐ problem(s) with artificial organs
- ☐ countries with the most transplants
- ☐ types of organs

PRESENTATION SKILL   Paraphrasing Experts to Support Opinions

LEARN

When you want to support your opinions, you can paraphrase the statements of experts, or the people who know a lot about the subject. When you paraphrase, you say something in your own words. There are several ways to paraphrase:

1. Use synonyms or expressions that mean the same thing.

   Artificial organs can save lives.

   People can live longer with man-made organs.

2. Use different word forms in the same family.

   People have a constant need for organs.

   People need organs constantly.

3. Use a different sentence structure.

   Because of a shortage of organs available for transplant, doctors must find other solutions.

   Doctors have to look for other solutions because there are never enough organs available for transplant.

Most people use more than one of these methods when they paraphrase.

APPLY

A. Work with a partner. Paraphrase each of the quotes below. Try to use each of the three ways to paraphrase mentioned in the Learn section. Use your dictionary for help if needed.

"One day soon, people will be able to live a long time with multiple artificial parts."

"Austin Whitney exceeded his own dreams when he walked across the stage at graduation."

B. Go online to listen to the discussion again. Write the paraphrase you hear about each topic.

1. A windpipe grown from pre-existing cells: *The doctor said*

   _____.

2. A new artificial heart in France: *The head of the American Medical*

   Association said _____.

3. Selling organs for transplant: *A professor at Harvard Medical School said*

   _____.

C. Write four different sentences about artificial organs or robotic technology. With a partner, take turns listening to each other's sentences and then paraphrasing them.

1. _____

2. _____

3. _____

4. _____

D. Choose a topic from one of the units in this book. What is your opinion on the topic? Prepare a three-minute talk on the topic and paraphrase ideas from one or more of the audios or videos. Present to a small group.

PRONUNCIATION SKILL | Chunking and Sentence Focus

LEARN

In every phrase or sentence, the most important word, the "focus word," is stressed. This word is usually the last content word and the easiest to hear. Highlighting the main idea in each phrase of a sentence is "sentence focus."

Remember that content words are typically nouns, main verbs, adjectives, and adverbs.

A. Listen to the sentences. Notice the focus words in pink.

1. The research is new.

2. Don't submit that.

B. Longer sentences have groups of words, or chunks. Good places to pause are after adverbial phrases, before prepositions and conjunctions, after items in a series, and after clauses. Go online to listen to the focus words in pink.

1. All of the options | are flexible | for students, | parents, | and teachers.

2. Why | are they at the hospital | if they are healthy?

C. Focus words can introduce new information. The old information is unstressed, and the new information is stressed. Listen to the following conversation. Notice the new information in pink.

A: My article was in the **journal**.

B: **Which** journal?

A: The **medical** journal published last month.

B: Did the journal receive **reviews**?

APPLY

A. Repeat the examples from Learn, activities A, B, and C. Stress the new information, pause when necessary, and use appropriate intonation.

B. With a partner, talk about a new medical technology that helps people do things that were impossible to do before. Ask questions about your partner's topic. Use proper sentence focus, pausing, and intonation.

A: I **learned** | that devices to help people **talk** | are becoming more **common**.

B: What do these devices **do**?

A: They record **words**, | **phrases**, | and **sentences**. | When they need to **communicate**, | they push a **button** | and the device **speaks**.

End of Unit Task

In this unit, you learned how to listen for reasons and explanations and how to paraphrase information to support an argument. Review these skills by choosing a topic and preparing arguments for and against the topic. As you review, paraphrase the information you find to support your argument.

A. Work in groups of four. Choose one of the three topics below. Two people will argue in favor of the topic and two people will argue against the topic.

> artificial brains (computers that think like people)
>
> People over the age of 70 receiving heart transplants
>
> personal robots for the disabled

B. Work with a partner to research your topic. Prepare a list of arguments and at least three reasons to support your position. For each argument, use information from experts to support your point of view. Paraphrase their ideas. Complete the graphic organizer.

Topic: Position: Reason	Expert information	Paraphrase

C. Meet with the other two people in your group. Discuss your topic. Whose argument was stronger? Who had more expert opinions? If necessary, do more research to make your position stronger. Use these questions to guide you.

1. Did you present three or more reasons for your position?
2. Did you support each reason with information from experts?
3. Did you paraphrase the information well?

D. With your group, debate your topic in front of the class or another group. Each side presents their arguments for two minutes. Decide whose arguments are stronger. Listen as other students debate their topics. Give feedback using the questions above in activity C.

Self-Assessment		
Yes	**No**	
☐	☐	I gave reasons for my position.
☐	☐	I supported each reason / argument with information from experts.
☐	☐	I paraphrased the expert's information.
☐	☐	I successfully listened for reasons and explanations.
☐	☐	I can use focus words to introduce new ideas.
☐	☐	I can use appropriate pausing and intonation.
☐	☐	I can correctly use the target vocabulary words from the unit.

Discussion Questions

With a partner or in a small group, discuss the following questions.

1. Do you think exoskeletons that allow disabled people to walk will become common?
2. Do you think scientists will be able to continue to create solutions for health issues?
3. Do you believe there is a limit to what scientists should create to fix health issues?

The Academic Word List

Words targeted in Level 1 are bold

Word	Sublist	Location
abandon	8	L2, U4
abstract	6	L3, U3
academy	5	L2, U10
access	4	L0, U5
accommodate	9	L3, U6
accompany	8	L4, U2
accumulate	8	L3, U4
accurate	6	L0, U2
achieve	2	L0, U4
acknowledge	6	L0, U7
acquire	2	L3, U9
adapt	7	L3, U7
adequate	4	L3, U9
adjacent	10	L4, U4
adjust	5	L4, U4
administrate	2	L4, U8
adult	7	L0, U10
advocate	7	L4, U3
affect	**2**	**L1, U1**
aggregate	6	L4, U6
aid	7	L0, U5
albeit	10	L4, U3
allocate	6	L3, U6
alter	5	L2, U6
alternative	**3**	**L1, U1**
ambiguous	8	L4, U7
amend	5	L4, U7
analogy	9	L4, U1
analyze	**1**	**L1, U3**
annual	**4**	**L1, U9**
anticipate	9	L2, U8
apparent	4	L2, U4
append	8	L4, U10
appreciate	8	L0, U9
approach	**1**	**L1, U1**
appropriate	2	L3, U5
approximate	4	L2, U7
arbitrary	8	L4, U7
area	1	L3, U7
aspect	2	L2, U7
assemble	10	L3, U1
assess	1	L2, U8
assign	6	L3, U5
assist	2	L0, U2
assume	1	L3, U1
assure	9	L4, U8
attach	6	L0, U10

Word	Sublist	Location
attain	9	L3, U5
attitude	4	L2, U4
attribute	4	L3, U8
author	6	L0, U1
authority	1	L2, U2
automate	8	L2, U1
available	1	L0, U8
aware	**5**	**L1, U1**
behalf	9	L4, U9
benefit	**1**	**L1, U2**
bias	8	L4, U3
bond	6	L4, U9
brief	6	L2, U9
bulk	9	L3, U1
capable	6	L3, U5
capacity	5	L3, U2
category	2	L2, U4
cease	9	L2, U2
challenge	**5**	**L1, U6**
channel	7	L4, U5
chapter	2	L0, U2
chart	8	L0, U2
chemical	7	L2, U6
circumstance	3	L4, U2
cite	6	L4, U4
civil	4	L3, U2
clarify	8	L3, U7
classic	7	L3, U6
clause	5	L4, U8
code	4	L0, U5
coherent	9	L4, U7
coincide	9	L4, U10
collapse	10	L3, U9
colleague	**10**	**L1, U5**
commence	9	L2, U4
comment	**3**	**L1, U4**
commission	2	L3, U2
commit	4	L2, U1
commodity	8	L4, U4
communicate	**4**	**L1, U3**
community	**2**	**L1, U4**
compatible	9	L2, U4
compensate	3	L4, U8
compile	10	L4, U9
complement	8	L4, U8

Oxford 3000™

Word	Sublist	Location
complex	2	L2, U1
component	3	L3, U1
compound	5	L3, U10
comprehensive	7	L2, U6
comprise	7	L3, U7
compute	**2**	**L1, U8**
conceive	10	L4, U7
concentrate	**4**	**L1, U5**
concept	1	L3, U10
conclude	2	L0, U6
concurrent	9	L4, U10
conduct	**2**	**L1, U4**
confer	4	L4, U8
confine	9	L4, U8
confirm	**7**	**L1, U8**
conflict	**5**	**L1, U7**
conform	8	L3, U6
consent	3	L3, U3
consequent	2	L4, U2
considerable	3	L4, U1
consist	**1**	**L1, U9**
constant	**3**	**L1, U8**
constitute	1	L4, U5
constrain	3	L4, U6
construct	2	L3, U1
consult	5	L2, U8
consume	2	L2, U6
contact	**5**	**L1, U4**
contemporary	8	L4, U6
context	1	L2, U4
contract	1	L3, U4
contradict	8	L2, U4
contrary	7	L3, U1
contrast	4	L3, U2
contribute	**3**	**L1, U9**
controversy	9	L2, U9
convene	3	L4, U1
converse	9	L2, U2
convert	7	L3, U3
convince	**10**	**L1, U5**
cooperate	6	L3, U6
coordinate	3	L2, U2
core	3	L4, U10
corporate	**3**	**L1, U7**
correspond	3	L2, U10
couple	7	L0, U4
create	1	L3, U7
credit	2	L2, U7
criteria	3	L3, U2
crucial	8	L3, U7
culture	2	L0, U10

Word	Sublist	Location
currency	8	L2, U3
cycle	4	L3, U5
data	1	L0, U4
debate	4	L3, U5
decade	**7**	**L1, U9**
decline	**5**	**L1, U9**
deduce	3	L4, U10
define	1	L0, U8
definite	7	L4, U8
demonstrate	**3**	**L1, U2**
denote	8	L4, U10
deny	**7**	**L1, U8**
depress	10	L0, U8
derive	1	L4, U8
design	2	L0, U10
despite	4	L3, U6
detect	8	L2, U3
deviate	8	L4, U10
device	9	L0, U2
devote	9	L2, U3
differentiate	7	L3, U6
dimension	4	L4, U9
diminish	9	L2, U8
discrete	5	L4, U2
discriminate	6	L4, U5
displace	8	L3, U10
display	6	L0, U8
dispose	7	L4, U1
distinct	2	L4, U2
distort	9	L4, U5
distribute	**1**	**L1, U9**
diverse	6	L3, U2
document	3	L0, U4
domain	6	L4, U6
domestic	4	L2, U5
dominate	3	L3, U7
draft	5	L0, U10
drama	8	L2, U9
duration	9	L2, U3
dynamic	7	L3, U3
economy	1	L2, U8
edit	**6**	**L1, U7**
element	2	L3, U1
eliminate	**7**	**L1, U6**
emerge	4	L3, U5
emphasis	**3**	**L1, U5**
empirical	7	L4, U4
enable	5	L2, U1
encounter	**10**	**L1, U8**

Word	Sublist	Location
energy	5	L0, U9
enforce	5	L4, U1
enhance	6	L3, U2
enormous	10	L0, U7
ensure	3	L4, U1
entity	5	L4, U8
environment	**1**	**L1, U1**
equate	2	L3, U10
equip	7	L2, U1
equivalent	**5**	**L1, U7**
erode	9	L4, U2
error	4	L0, U2
establish	1	L2, U5
estate	6	L4, U8
estimate	1	L2, U5
ethic	9	L3, U4
ethnic	4	L3, U9
evaluate	**2**	**L1, U8**
eventual	8	L3, U2
evident	1	L2, U8
evolve	5	L2, U2
exceed	**6**	**L1, U10**
exclude	3	L3, U8
exhibit	8	L2, U3
expand	5	L0, U5
expert	6	L0, U3
explicit	6	L4, U3
exploit	8	L4, U9
export	1	L4, U6
expose	5	L4, U1
external	5	L2, U1
extract	7	L3, U1
facilitate	5	L3, U6
factor	1	L3, U1
feature	2	L0, U2
federal	6	L4, U4
fee	6	L0, U5
file	7	L0, U5
final	2	L0, U1
finance	1	L3, U6
finite	7	L4, U9
flexible	**6**	**L1, U10**
fluctuate	8	L4, U10
focus	2	L0, U6
format	9	L2, U8
formula	1	L3, U5
forthcoming	10	L4, U10
found	9	L0, U7
foundation	**7**	**L1, U9**
framework	3	L4, U6

Word	Sublist	Location
function	1	L3, U3
fund	3	L2, U5
fundamental	**5**	**L1, U8**
furthermore	6	L3, U4
gender	6	L3, U8
generate	**5**	**L1, U5**
generation	5	L2, U10
globe	7	L2, U5
goal	4	L0, U7
grade	7	L0, U3
grant	4	L3, U9
guarantee	**7**	**L1, U7**
guideline	**8**	**L1, U6**
hence	4	L3, U6
hierarchy	7	L4, U6
highlight	8	L0, U7
hypothesis	4	L3, U4
identical	7	L3, U3
identify	**1**	**L1, U3**
ideology	7	L4, U3
ignorance	6	L2, U9
illustrate	3	L0, U1
image	**5**	**L1, U3**
immigrate	3	L4, U7
impact	2	L2, U9
implement	4	L4, U2
implicate	4	L4, U3
implicit	8	L4, U3
imply	3	L3, U8
impose	4	L3, U10
incentive	6	L4, U2
incidence	6	L3, U4
incline	10	L4, U4
income	1	L0, U4
incorporate	6	L4, U9
index	6	L4, U9
indicate	1	L2, U10
individual	1	L0, U1
induce	8	L4, U1
inevitable	8	L3, U2
infer	7	L4, U3
infrastructure	8	L4, U1
inherent	9	L4, U7
inhibit	6	L4, U2
initial	3	L0, U3
initiate	6	L3, U8
injure	2	L4, U9
innovate	7	L3, U1

Oxford 3000™

Word	Sublist	Location
input	6	L2, U5
insert	7	L2, U7
insight	9	L3, U4
inspect	8	L4, U9
instance	3	L3, U3
institute	**2**	**L1, U6**
instruct	**6**	**L1, U6**
integral	9	L4, U6
integrate	4	L4, U6
integrity	10	L2, U1
intelligence	6	L0, U10
intense	8	L3, U7
interact	3	L2, U3
intermediate	9	L2, U5
internal	**4**	**L1, U10**
interpret	1	L3, U10
interval	6	L3, U10
intervene	7	L3, U6
intrinsic	10	L4, U7
invest	2	L3, U2
investigate	4	L2, U9
invoke	10	L4, U5
involve	1	L3, U7
isolate	7	L3, U2
issue	1	L0, U3
item	2	L0, U6
job	4	L0, U10
journal	**2**	**L1, U10**
justify	3	L4, U2
label	4	L0, U1
labor	1	L2, U4
layer	3	L3, U3
lecture	6	L0, U6
legal	**1**	**L1, U2**
legislate	1	L4, U1
levy	10	L4, U3
liberal	5	L4, U3
license	5	L3, U8
likewise	10	L3, U4
link	3	L0, U4
locate	**3**	**L1, U4**
logic	5	L3, U5
maintain	**2**	**L1, U10**
major	1	L3, U7
manipulate	8	L4, U10
manual	9	L3, U10
margin	5	L2, U3
mature	9	L2, U8

Word	Sublist	Location
maximize	**3**	**L1, U9**
mechanism	4	L3, U3
media	7	L0, U8
mediate	9	L4, U10
medical	**5**	**L1, U2**
medium	**9**	**L1, U10**
mental	5	L2, U6
method	**1**	**L1, U2**
migrate	6	L4, U1
military	9	L2, U3
minimal	**9**	**L1, U9**
minimize	8	L3, U1
minimum	**6**	**L1, U10**
ministry	6	L4, U6
minor	3	L0, U7
mode	7	L4, U5
modify	**5**	**L1, U6**
monitor	5	L3, U4
motive	6	L2, U7
mutual	9	L2, U2
negate	3	L4, U4
network	5	L2, U2
neutral	6	L2, U5
nevertheless	6	L3, U5
nonetheless	10	L4, U5
norm	9	L4, U7
normal	2	L0, U6
notion	5	L3, U5
notwithstanding	10	L4, U6
nuclear	8	L3, U9
objective	5	L0, U4
obtain	2	L3, U4
obvious	**4**	**L1, U7**
occupy	4	L4, U8
occur	1	L2, U10
odd	**10**	**L1, U8**
offset	8	L4, U9
ongoing	10	L2, U7
option	**4**	**L1, U10**
orient	5	L4, U4
outcome	3	L2, U7
output	4	L2, U5
overall	4	L2, U9
overlap	9	L2, U4
overseas	6	L2, U3
panel	10	L4, U5
paradigm	7	L4, U2
paragraph	**8**	**L1, U7**

Oxford 3000™

Word	Sublist	Location
🔑 parallel	4	L4, U3
parameter	4	L3, U4
🔑 **participate**	**2**	**L1, U2**
🔑 partner	3	L0, U3
passive	9	L3, U10
perceive	2	L3, U7
🔑 **percent**	**1**	**L1, U3**
🔑 period	1	L3, U3
persist	10	L3, U4
🔑 perspective	5	L2, U10
🔑 phase	4	L2, U10
phenomenon	7	L4, U4
🔑 philosophy	3	L3, U8
🔑 physical	3	L0, U1
🔑 plus	8	L0, U6
🔑 policy	1	L2, U9
portion	9	L2, U6
🔑 pose	10	L4, U4
🔑 positive	2	L0, U7
🔑 potential	2	L2, U10
practitioner	8	L4, U1
precede	6	L3, U9
🔑 precise	5	L3, U3
🔑 predict	4	L0, U9
predominant	8	L4, U5
preliminary	9	L2, U2
presume	6	L4, U7
🔑 previous	2	L0, U9
🔑 **primary**	**2**	**L1, U3**
prime	5	L4, U2
🔑 principal	4	L2, U10
🔑 principle	1	L3, U10
🔑 prior	4	L2, U8
🔑 priority	7	L2, U6
🔑 proceed	1	L2, U1
🔑 **process**	**1**	**L1, U2**
🔑 **professional**	**4**	**L1, U2**
prohibit	7	L3, U2
🔑 **project**	**4**	**L1, U9**
🔑 promote	4	L4, U7
🔑 proportion	3	L2, U8
🔑 prospect	8	L4, U6
protocol	9	L4, U9
psychology	5	L2, U8
🔑 publication	7	L3, U9
🔑 publish	3	L0, U1
🔑 purchase	2	L0, U7
🔑 pursue	5	L4, U4
qualitative	9	L4, U8
🔑 **quote**	**7**	**L1, U7**

Word	Sublist	Location
radical	8	L4, U5
random	8	L2, U5
🔑 range	2	L2, U10
ratio	5	L3, U10
rational	6	L3, U9
🔑 **react**	**3**	**L1, U3**
🔑 recover	6	L2, U1
refine	9	L3, U5
regime	4	L3, U9
🔑 region	2	L2, U2
🔑 register	3	L3, U8
regulate	2	L2, U2
reinforce	8	L3, U4
🔑 **reject**	**5**	**L1, U10**
🔑 relax	9	L0, U6
🔑 release	7	L2, U5
🔑 relevant	2	L3, U8
reluctant	10	L2, U3
🔑 rely	3	L2, U9
🔑 remove	3	L0, U9
🔑 require	1	L0, U10
🔑 research	1	L0, U3
reside	2	L4, U3
🔑 resolve	4	L2, U4
🔑 resource	2	L0, U3
🔑 **respond**	**1**	**L1, U4**
🔑 restore	8	L2, U10
restrain	9	L3, U9
🔑 restrict	2	L2, U7
🔑 retain	4	L4, U7
🔑 reveal	6	L2, U1
revenue	5	L3, U6
🔑 reverse	7	L3, U9
🔑 **revise**	**8**	**L1, U7**
🔑 revolution	9	L3, U3
rigid	9	L2, U6
🔑 role	1	L0, U9
🔑 route	9	L3, U9
scenario	9	L2, U7
🔑 **schedule**	**7**	**L1, U5**
scheme	3	L3, U2
scope	6	L2, U9
🔑 section	1	L0, U9
🔑 sector	1	L4, U6
🔑 **secure**	**2**	**L1, U6**
🔑 seek	2	L2, U7
🔑 **select**	**2**	**L1, U4**
sequence	**3**	**L1, U6**
🔑 series	4	L0, U9
🔑 sex	3	L4, U4

🔑 Oxford 3000™

Word	Sublist	Location
shift	3	L2, U7
significant	1	L3, U2
similar	**1**	**L1, U5**
simulate	7	L3, U4
site	2	L0, U5
so-called	10	L2, U9
sole	7	L4, U10
somewhat	7	L3, U7
source	**1**	**L1, U1**
specific	**1**	**L1, U6**
specify	**3**	**L1, U8**
sphere	9	L4, U6
stable	5	L3, U10
statistic	4	L3, U8
status	4	L0, U4
straightforward	10	L3, U6
strategy	2	L2, U2
stress	4	L3, U7
structure	1	L2, U1
style	5	L2, U2
submit	**7**	**L1, U10**
subordinate	9	L4, U3
subsequent	4	L3, U5
subsidy	6	L4, U8
substitute	5	L2, U3
successor	7	L3, U6
sufficient	3	L4, U2
sum	4	L3, U9
summary	**4**	**L1, U3**
supplement	9	L2, U6
survey	2	L2, U6
survive	7	L2, U9
suspend	9	L4, U5
sustain	5	L3, U1
symbol	5	L0, U8
tape	6	L3, U8
target	5	L2, U6
task	3	L0, U5
team	9	L0, U3
technical	3	L3, U3
technique	3	L3, U5
technology	3	L2, U10
temporary	9	L0, U8
tense	7	L2, U6
terminate	7	L4, U10
text	2	L0, U1
theme	**7**	**L1, U5**
theory	1	L3, U8
thereby	7	L4, U7
thesis	7	L4, U7

Word	Sublist	Location
topic	7	L0, U6
trace	6	L4, U5
tradition	2	L0, U2
transfer	**2**	**L1, U6**
transform	6	L3, U1
transit	5	L2, U8
transmit	7	L4, U1
transport	**6**	**L1, U1**
trend	**5**	**L1, U4**
trigger	9	L4, U1
ultimate	7	L3, U8
undergo	10	L4, U9
underlie	6	L4, U5
undertake	4	L4, U2
uniform	7	L2, U4
unify	9	L2, U5
unique	7	L3, U10
utilize	6	L3, U1
valid	3	L3, U8
vary	1	L2, U1
vehicle	**7**	**L1, U1**
version	**5**	**L1, U7**
via	7	L4, U4
violate	9	L4, U3
virtual	8	L3, U3
visible	7	L2, U6
vision	9	L0, U8
visual	8	L3, U7
volume	**3**	**L1, U8**
voluntary	7	L3, U10
welfare	5	L4, U9
whereas	5	L4, U5
whereby	10	L4, U10
widespread	7	L2, U3

Oxford 3000™